THEOLOGY
in the
WESLEYAN SPIRIT

THEOLOGY
in the
WESLEYAN SPIRIT

ALBERT C. OUTLER

TIDINGS   NASHVILLE

tidings

Library of Congress Catalog Card Number:
74–24509

EV021B

CONTENTS

FOREWORD

ALBERT OUTLER has aptly described Mr. Wesley as a
"folk theologian." Wesley wrote theology for the common people to whom he preached, and his teachings
were geared to their level of comprehension and understanding. His audience would have been the television
audience, if there had been television in the eighteenth
century and if it had been as readily accessible to the
masses as it is today. Indeed, he disseminated his theology
in tracts, not full-length books, and the demand for those
tracts was such that invariably he made money off them.
His publications were forerunners of the paperbacks of
our post-war era.

"I now write," Mr. Wesley asserted, "as I generally
speak, *ad populum* ('to the bulk of mankind'), to those
who neither relish nor understand the act of speaking,
but who, notwithstanding, are competent judges of those
truths which are necessary to present and future happiness—I design plain truth for plain people."

Dr. Outler, in expounding Wesley's theology, like a dutiful disciple, has successfully imitated the Master's example. His book is clear and simply, as well as elegantly composed. His reading public is the common lot of Christian people in the English-speaking world. One does not have to be tutored in theology to understand and appreciate the theology he here sets forth.

His earlier book *Evangelism in the Wesleyan Spirit* was an attempt to show Methodists how to evangelize today with the earnestness, conviction, and reliance with which John Wesley evangelized with such remarkable success in the eighteenth century. In this book he attempts to show us how to gain an adequate theological understanding and to express our theological convictions in a meaningful and convincing way to others by expounding Wesley's basic theological ideas and translating them into contemporary usage.

The first chapter is a delineation of Wesley's wise use of contemporary eighteenth century secular thought in the promotion of the gospel. Father John despoiled the enemies of Christianity of all their goods as the Israelites did the Egyptians as they left Egypt at the time of the Exodus. Chapter two is a remarkable modernization of Wesley's doctrine of original sin. Chapter three is a beautiful deliniation of the work of Christ in Wesleyan perspective. And chapter four tells us most convincingly that Wesley's precept of perfect love in this life still holds and shall be the burden of our concern now as it was his in the eighteenth century. Without it, social schemes of reconstruction and plans for the improvement of human-kind are superficial and, in the end, ineffective.

What Dr. Outler has done in this little book is a remarkable achievement. It is another gem in the crown of his gifted contribution to Wesleyan theology and is a noble tribute to the enduring quality of Mr. Wesley's theology.

Methodists and non-Methodists alike can profit from this little book.

William R. Cannon, Resident Bishop
The Atlanta Area
The United Methodist Church

1

"PLUNDERING THE EGYPTIANS"

FOUR YEARS AGO, I tried my hand at translating my researches in Wesley into an updated interpretation of *Evangelism in the Wesleyan Spirit*.[1] That, by definition, was only a partial view of the man and his work (albeit at the beating heart of it all). Now, I'm concerned to enlarge our angle of vision somewhat and to propose another interpretive sketch of Wesley this time *as a signficant theologian* whose importance as theologian, then and now, has been badly underestimated by both his devotées and critics. He was, I have come to believe, the most important Anglican theologian in his century. He is, I also believe, a very considerable resource in our own time for *our* theological reflections, especially for those who have any serious interest in the ecumenical dialogue and in the cause of Christian unity. My aim and hope is to help rescue Wesley from his status as cult-hero to the Methodists (by whom he has been revered but not carefully studied) and to exhibit him as a creative Christian thinker with a special word for *these* parlous times and for us, as we try to grapple with the new problems created by the current crises in culture—problems posed by the passing of all the old polarities (Protestant–Catholic–"Enlightenment," etc.) that served to define so many of our received traditions, now eroded or eroding. For better or for worse, we are at the end of that cultural syndrome once defined by: (1) the Renaissance–Enlightenment concern for form and reason; (2) the Protestant Reformation's insistence upon *sola fide;* (3) the Roman Counter Reformation's alternative of an authoritarian church–culture; (4) the mores of a deferential society that supported patterns and codes of *ex officio* authority; (5) the dominance of European–North American culture; (6) soaring faith in science and technology; and (7) the idea of human progress. It is, therefore, a baffling time, a difficult time in which to proclaim the good news of God in Christ as credible and relevant. And yet—although our circumstances are radically different from Wesley's—it is just exactly the sort of crisis that he would have tried heroically to comprehend, confident that the perennial gospel still offers to us in the twentieth century the same eternal truth and hope he himself had proved it had for eighteenth century Englishmen: not only the lively hope of *heaven,* but also a credible hope for a meaningful life in *this* age (and any age) whatever its crises between theology and culture. At any rate, this is my agenda in the following chapters.

Wesley the evangelist is, of course, a familiar figure (actually a stereotype), and so also Wesley the organizer, and even Wesley the social reformer who helped shape a reformation of morals and manners in British life.[2] But what has gone largely obscured is *Wesley the theologian* —specifically, a theologian of culture and, even more specifically, a *folk-theologian* who found effective ways to communicate the gospel to mass audiences who cared little about the complexity of his sources or the cultural import of his evangelistic messages.

Where we must begin, therefore, is with Wesley's eclectic heritage and lifestyle, as a man and as a theologian. He was born into a home where piety and culture had long been blended as a matter of course. He learned to read early and he continued to read and study incessantly throughout a long and busy life. His tastes ranged over the entire literary spectrum, from the classics to what were, in his day, the newest essays, novels, plays, and treatises. It was no accident that he was a favored friend of Dr. Johnson's (the literary panjandrum of Augustan England).[3] He was, moreover, equally concerned with political history and current social change.[4] His lifespan coincided in a remarkable way with a period in British history that turned out to be its prelude to modernity— so that almost without knowing it, Wesley faced both ways in a bewildering ambivalence (toward the European past that he understood so well and toward the global future that he glimpsed with remarkable prescience). It was, as we know, a great age in the history of science, and Wesley was keenly interested in this—"the latest scientific discoveries," and all that—confident that every advance into scientific truth would reveal "the wisdom of God in creation"[5] to the eyes of faith.

All of which is intended to remind us that Wesley, like most Christian thinkers before him (back to St. Paul), had to grapple with the problem of what we have come to call "secularism": viz., how are the treasures of human culture to be related to and appropriated by a credible Christian theology that appreciates humane wisdom wherever found—without forfeiting its own integrity? Wesley's eclecticism had an honorable history, with great trailblazers before him, whom he knew. There was Origen, the very first Christian theologian with a first-rate classical education. In Exodus 12:18–36 there is that strange story about the departing Israelites applying to their erstwhile Egyptian masters for "gifts." Moreover, says the Exodus historian, "the Lord made the Egyptians well-disposed toward the Israelites and let them have whatever they asked. In this way, they [the Israelites] plundered the Egyptians." A man as sensitive to biblical morality as Origen was bound to feel queasy with such a story (it does sound a bit like ripping off, doesn't it?). And so he came up with an imaginative allegory. "Plundering the Egyptians," he explained, is a *metaphor,* pointing to the freedom that Christians have (by divine allowance) to explore, appraise, and appropriate all the insights and resources of any and all secular culture. Later, St. Augustine, in his *De Doctrina Christiana* would borrow this metaphor as *his* warrant for Christian transvaluations of classical culture.[6] The thoughtful Christian who understands the live core of the gospel and who is deep-rooted in the biblical witness to God's self-revelation is thereby entitled and encouraged to exploit the full range of secular literature, science, and philosophy—always with a view to the enrichment of one's Christian wisdom and the enhancement of his effectiveness in communicating the Christian message. The richer one's "Egyptian plunder" (i.e., one's secular culture) the richer one's understanding of God's wisdom and power in Christ —who, as Logos and Light, is the true illumination for all seekers after truth and wisdom.[7]

This is one of the best of our Christian traditions—evangelical Christians reaching out to discern and evaluate secular wisdoms of every sort. And this is why any theology that is content to be exclusively biblic*ist*, or traditional*ist*, is invalid and finally fruitless—just as, on the other side, any theology without an evangelical focus will soon drown in its surrounding secular milieu. And when you stop to think how much of Christian thought and teaching nowadays tends toward simplistic biblic*ism*, over on the right wing, and Pelagian secular*ism*, on the left (or, sometimes, professedly "traditional*ist*" but with only a shallow, thin "tradition"), one wonders if any further explanation is required for the all too obvious cultural impoverishment of so many of our pulpits and pews.

And just as Wesley understood and practiced this art of "plundering the Egyptians"—their arts and letters, their philosophy and science, their political and moral insights—so also he challenges us to go and do likewise. But we had better take careful note as to how skillfully he managed it—so that his immense erudition never obscured his "plain words for those plain people" who were his primary audiences by his own choice. He was one of the few truly successful popularizers in the history of preaching who never beguiled his audiences and who rarely oversimplified real issues. His preaching and teaching offered both the gospel *and* a liberal education, as an integrated experience, to the common people who heard him gladly. What a tragedy, then, that this art of "plundering the Egyptians" (without remaining in Egypt!) has been so sadly neglected in our time: so that now we have evangelicals with very little humane culture to speak of, on one side, and, over on the other, liberals and secularizers with no deep rootage in the Bible and no strong resonance with the mind of Christ in Scripture.

It would, therefore, be worth taking a closer look at Wesley's actual practice of the art. He recorded most of his reading after 1725,[8] and this record runs to more than fourteen hundred different authors, with nearly three thousand separate items from them (ranging from pamphlets to twelve-volume sets—including many huge leather bound folios: sermons, histories, geography, voyages, and travels). He had had, as we sometimes forget, a rich classical education and he kept this furbished and in use throughout his whole career. His quotations— from the classics or wherever—are rarely identified and rarely exact. And they do sound a bit odd in our ears in what appear as sermons for mass audiences.[9] Do you suppose, maybe, that mass audiences can take more "culture" than we have condescendingly supposed (or are actually prepared to offer them)? At any rate, we have managed thus far, in the sermons alone, to identify twenty-seven quotations from Horace, many of them repeated in different sermons.[10] Virgil follows with nine-teen,[11] Ovid with ten, Cicero with nine, and Juvenal seven. Twelve other classical authors [12] show up, repeat-edly whenever they can serve, in support (but sometimes also mere decoration) of one interesting point or another. Wesley's other "classical" sources range from Plato to Aristotle to Plotinus to Augustine to à Kempis. He knows the medieval mystics and the Renaissance secular-ists (e.g., Rabelais). He quotes freely from Shakespeare (once referring to him as "our heathen poet" [13]) and from Milton even more freely—but also from Abraham Cowley, George Herbert, Thomas Parnell, and Matthew Prior. He had read widely in patristic theology, was well-grounded in the Reformation classics but was even more intimately acquainted with English "divinity," from Hooker to Baxter to Tillotson and Doddridge. His special anthology of "British divinity" appears, "extracted," in *A Christian Library*, but this is no more than a slice of a vaster bibliography to which he had exposed himself. One thing, therefore, is clear: if anybody proposes to theologize "in the Wesleyan spirit," he must learn to read and to *love* to read, to remember and to reflect—about all sorts of events and ideas in our human heritage and in our current world—as if he, too, were driven by the compulsions of an inquiring mind as Wesley was.

But literature was not the whole story of Wesley's culture by any means. He read all the "modern science" he could lay his hands on, with one eye on its theological import, and the other on its practical applications.[14] He had informed opinions about Newton and he soaked up the great popularizers of science in his day (Ray,

Derham, Buddaeus, Goldsmith, and others) always supposing that whatever was true would help to illuminate
God's glory in and through *his* creation. What often
strikes one as odd, given our image of Wesley the evangelist, is the way in which he can comment on secular
insights (especially in the later sermons) with no explicit
evangelical reference for them (even though the biblical
world-view is everywhere presupposed as self-evident).
There are even some intriguing "off-limit" quotations
(as a puritan might regard them) that expose his exten-
sive acquaintance with English drama (including Restoration melodrama)—even while he was also denouncing
the English theatre as a sinkhole of iniquity. For example,
in 1726 he read Thomas Otway's *The Orphan, or the
Unhappy Marriage*, written in 1680.[15] In 1759, one of
the more telling quotations in Wesley's sermon on "Original Sin" is from Otway's *The Orphan*, Act V, Scene 1
(but, of course, with no citation). Now, did he keep that
particular quotation in his head for thirty years; was
it in his notes; or, had he reread Otway in the interim?
I wish I knew. What is certain is that very few of his
readers—then or since—have ever recognized the source
of this quotation (or dozens like it). It was something
of a detective feat for us to find it—and I use the pro-
noun *us* here quite literally, for in my search for these
sources of Wesley's myriad uncited quotations, I have
had the invaluable aid of Mrs. John Warnick[16] and
Mrs. Wanda Smith (my research assistant).

All of this, however, was no more than an impressive
superstructure set firmly upon a massive foundation of
biblical learning, plus an incredible "information retrie-

val system" that reveals Wesley as a sort of walking
concordance plus commentary, all in one. It was his
profound sense of the Bible as a "speaking book" that
gave him his freedom to "plunder the Egyptians" and
guided him in the use he made of their treasures. One
of the influences of the Holy Club on him was their
collective emphasis upon Scripture as the primal authority
that stands above and beyond all polarities and confes-
sional formularies. In a letter to John Newton, April 24,
1765, Wesley says, "In 1730 I began to be *homo unius
libri,* to study (comparatively) no book but the Bible." [17]
In his preface to his first collection of *Sermons on
Several Occasions* (1746) he avows his intention to be
homo unius libri ("a man of just one book").[18] That
"one book," of course, was Scripture and there can be
no doubt at all that Wesley was, intentionally and in fact,
a biblical man. All his basic insights are rooted in, or
derived from, the Scriptures; he would often appeal "to
the Law and the Testimony" as his court of last resort;[19]
he would often urge his readers to weigh a difficult
question "in the balance of the sanctuary" [i.e., in
prayerful reflection upon the biblical data].[20] By *sola
Scriptura* ("Scripture alone") he never meant "*nothing
but Scripture,*" just as by *unius libri* he never meant to
exclude other books from his reading list—as we have
already seen. But he did mean that Scripture was his first
and final norm for the validation of any theological discussion. This meant a lifelong, total immersion in Scripture: in its original languages, in its dominant themes
and images, in all its parts and in its organic wholeness.
It was just this conviction that the Scripture insights are

integral throughout, as a chorused witness to God's grace and human need, that allowed Wesley to range at will over the entire Bible and to conflate texts and paraphrases from here and there in sentences of his own in ways that are next to unimaginable to us nowadays—but that are neither unintelligible nor artificial (strange as that may seem). To verify this generalization experimentally, let me test it on you. Here are two (consecutive) sentences from his sermon on "Original Sin" (the one with the Otway quote mentioned above):

> The Scripture avers, that by one man's disobedience, all men were constituted sinners; that in Adam all died, spiritually died, lost the life and the image of God; that fallen, sinful Adam then begat a son in his own likeness; nor was it possible he should beget him in any other, for who can bring a clean thing out of an unclean? That, consequently, we as well as other men, were by nature, dead in treaspasses and sins, without hope, without God in the world, and therefore children of wrath; [so] that every man may say, I was shapen in wickedness, and in sin did my mother conceive me; that there is no difference, in that all have sinned, and come short of the glory of God, of that glorious image of God, wherein man was originally created.21

Now, obviously, you can recognize that this language is, indeed, "biblical," but does it read as if it were "scissored-and-pasted"? Did you recognize that this passage, in its entirety, is composed of bits and pieces from Roman 5:19, 1 Corinthians 15:22, Genesis 5:3, Job 14:4, Ephesians 2: 1, 12, and 3, Psalm 51:5, and then back home to Romans 3:22–23, in *that* order?

Let's try one more sample of this sort of thing that came to be a commonplace in Wesley's rhetoric (in his sermons, essays, letters, and treatises). There are hundreds of others like it that you can check out for yourself if you're interested—as I've come to be.

> We are enabled by the Spirit to mortify the deeds of the body, of our evil nature; and as we are more and more dead to sin, we are more and more alive to God. We go on from grace to grace, while we are careful to abstain from all appearance of evil, and are zealous of good works as we have opportunity, doing good to all men, while we walk in all His ordinances blameless, therein worshipping Him in spirit and in truth, while we take up our cross, and deny ourselves every pleasure that does not lead us to God.[22]

What this adds up to is an obvious but crucial conclusion: Wesley *lived* in the Scriptures and his mind ranged over the Bible's length and breadth and depth like a radar, tuned into the pertinent data on every point he cared to make.

And yet this business of living in Scripture was not really what we have come to call "proof-texting" (i.e., the mechanical use of Scripture texts in support of some thesis or other that may or may not be truly "biblical," in its full context). Actually, these were only a few great basic themes that Wesley had discerned as the nerve centers of the biblical revelation and they guided him in both exegesis and hermeneutics. This becomes apparent as soon as you lay out all his recorded texts in various patterns and combinations. As some of you may know,

Wesley kept a "Sermon Register" from 1747 to 1761. We have extended this to include every mention of any sermon and text anywhere else in the Wesley corpus and then have tried to organize these data into charts and generalizations that apply to his oral preaching as well as to his written sermons (published and manuscript). We are not at all certain that we yet have the full record: our 13,739 recorded texts fall short of the 40,000 some odd sermons attributed to him in his lifetime by some 26,000—in other words, by some two-thirds. Still, it must be the most nearly complete inventory of such statistics in existence and our efforts to analyze them are proving fruitful in many ways. For example, consider the text he used most often, 190 times: "Repent ye, and believe the gospel" (Mark 1:15). Then, combine that with Isaiah 55:6 and 55:7, "Seek ye the Lord while he may be found. . . . Let the wicked forsake his way, and the unrighteous man his thoughts: and let him return unto the Lord, and he will have mercy upon him; and to our God, for he will abundantly *pardon*," 90 and 112 times, respectively (i.e., 202 times together). Their sum (392 times) clearly suggests that Wesley's prime concern was the gospel call to repentance and the promise of pardon (and, remember that Isaiah was "gospel," too!). Look then at the next cluster of his overall favorites: (1) 2 Corinthians 8:9, "For ye know the grace of our Lord Jesus Christ, that, though he was rich, yet for your sakes he became poor, that ye through his poverty might be rich" (167 times); (2) Ephesians 2:8, "For by grace are ye saved through faith; and that not of yourselves: it is the gift of God" (133 times);

and (3) Galatians 6:14, "But God forbid that I should glory, save in the cross of our Lord Jesus Christ, by whom the world is crucified unto me, and I unto the world" (129 times). From this it becomes evident that, for Wesley, the call to repentance was always linked with the gospel's offer of reconciliation through Christ and salvation by grace. His first six favorite texts, then, are all variations on the central evangelical message: *repent and accept God's grace in Christ!* There are many other fascinating patterns that have turned up in the course of our analyses of these texts—e.g., Wesley's favorite text in the first half-year of the Revival (1739) was 1 Corinthians 1:30, "But of him are ye in Christ Jesus, who of God is made unto us wisdom, and righteousness, and sanctification, and redemption" (12 times), and this was followed by Acts 16:30b, "What must I do to be saved?" (10 times). The following year (1740) his favorite text is the sixth chapter of Matthew (i.e., the central section of the Sermon on the Mount): 10 times. In 1741, his favorite text was Ephesians 2:8, "For by grace are ye saved through faith" (10 times). The New Testament books he preached from most often were Matthew (1,362 times), Hebrews (965 times) and John (910 times)—and he records no preaching texts from Philemon or 0 John. In the Old Testament Isaiah ranks first (668 times), Psalms second (624 times) and Jeremiah third (208 times), and he has left no record of ever having preached from the books of Ezra, Esther, Song of Solomon, Obadiah, or Nahum.

This (and much else I could lay out if space and time were no object) confirms the sincerity of Wesley's intention to live in the Bible as his theological climate. But this was matched by a comparable concern that his people also learn to live in and by the Scriptures in much the same way. For it was the interplay between Wesley's citations of Scripture and his people's familiarity with Scripture (however elementary) that so strongly reinforced the dynamics of his preaching and its impact. When a preacher has only a limited background in Scripture texts pondered deeply enough to support real biblical preaching and when his people have even less (or else a contrary hermeneutics), then one of the essential preconditions of effective Christian communication is missing—and this is enough in itself to account for many of our failures in effective pulpit communication today.

What I've been trying to suggest thus far is that Wesley was very much a man of his own time and yet also that his interest in the relevance of the perennial gospel in the constantly changing human situation is pertinent to our own efforts to update that same gospel and to relate it, as best we may, to the vast and radical crises of our times. One does not presume to stipulate exactly how Wesley would have diagnosed this current age. There is no doubt, however, that he would have *undertaken* a diagnosis, and we can suggest some of the fundamental principles he would have taken for his guidelines. At the heart of it all, then and now, is the overarching issue that defined Christianity's crisis in the eighteenth century and that, in similar fashion, defines the crisis in which we are floundering in this latter half of the twentieth century: viz., human autonomy (freedom) versus heteronomy (oppression) on the one side (the human claim to our own control of our human destiny) and, over against these, Christian *theo*-nomy of one sort or another (human life lived intentionally by the righteousness and grace of God). In Wesley's day, the deists and French *philosophes* were the partisans of autonomy while secular tyrannies in variety represented the ancient traditions of social and political oppression. Wesley opposed both autonomy *and* heteronomy and sought instead a spiritual and social revolution in which *theo*-nomy provided both worldview and lifestyle for Christians: the love of God above all else and all else in God, reverence toward God, and the dignity of grace to *all* his children.

In our day—when all the great traditions that have held the world together for centuries (however tenuously) are suddenly becoming frazzled and "inoperative" —the issue between human self-sufficiency and God's primacy is still the great dividing line in all our struggles for a theology of culture that is actually *theo*-logy and not some sort of religious *anthro*-pology writ large across a cosmic backdrop. All our most fashionable credos today (the new a-morality, the new secularism, the new emotionalism and "supernaturalisms"—ESP, psychokinesis, "transcendental meditation," TA, and others) are all fresh variations on the old themes of human autonomy: viz., the conviction that human beings can and must accept final responsibility for their own well-being and their collective destinies. God, in this view, is at best a cosmic coach and, at worst, a pious fiction. Self-salvation is the implicit claim of all the self-help movements of our time

—and not a few of the popular religious movements as well. But human autonomy, even partially achieved, attracts a counteraction from the right (viz., the management of our human affairs by other human beings— which is a working definition of heteronomy). Thus we may venture into prophecy: when a society that has been enchanted by the visions of self-salvation becomes disenchanted (or comes under the sorts of social and economic duress we are now experiencing), that society is sadly vulnerable to secular tyranny. For anyone to fail to see that *this* is the agonizing issue at the heart of our progressive disintegration as a nation for the past two decades is a strange form of moral blindness. What is worse, the choice between autonomy and heteronomy is humanly intolerable in the long run. Autonomy is a delusion and heteronomy is a degradation. Is this what folk like Solzhenitsyn have been trying to tell us?

It is, therefore, clearly in the Wesleyan spirit for Christians (ministers and laity alike) to explore the terms in which God's primacy and sovereign grace may once again be affirmed and translated into convincing witness and service in this world as it exists and as it runs its course. But, even supposing that we could, in reasonable measure, master this ancient art of plundering the Egyptians, how on earth would we put such resources to fruitful use?

There is no easy answer here. Christian ministers in our day, as we know all too well, are struggling in the throes of a deep identity crisis. They are no longer "the parsons" of their town or city and thus are no longer decisively influential in public affairs, *ex officio*. But if they turn, in desperation or relief, to some other sort of service profession—as "public relations persons," amateur journalists or editors, paramedical "shrinks," or even professors—they are still without a truly distinctive "office," with no indispensable *professional* rôle in this new society of ours. Whatever such amateurs can do, in those various rôles and functions, professionals can do as well or better. But what none of them can do as well as good ministers, who really know their calling (who understand its resources in Scripture and tradition together with its art of transvaluating secular wisdoms into Christian insights), is to bring the gospel to bear on the living, aching concerns of contemporary men and women in their daily round, in the terms of their specific current cultural perceptions. The only really distinctive thing the Christian minister has to offer—in its appropriate cultural context—is the Christian gospel in its full essence, replete with its promises to transform and hallow human lives and human culture. The fundamentalist or liberal who is either antipathetic to a given current culture or out of touch with it—no matter how devout, or "biblical," or ecstatic or "activist"—cannot really do this. The impact of such "sectarians" on history and on society is either marginal or short lived. But the *evangelical* Christian must also have an ample grasp and evaluation of the culture and times in which one lives (a vivid sense of tradition—the human past— together with a realistic sense of the human prospect). This is one's "Egyptian plunder" and one must take careful, constant thought as to how it may be exploited most effectively in preaching and teaching—else one will not be preaching the *full* gospel, either, no matter what one's advertising "logo" may be.

This, or something like it, is what Wesley understood as "theological education" and what he insisted on from his preachers, ignoring their general lack of *formal* education. His first question was always about a person's "gifts, graces, and fruits"—one's commitment to Christ and to the Scriptures' witness as God's Word and our Savior. But he then also asked about each person's willingness to learn and his/her aptness for study and teaching. His curriculum for "continuing education" would certainly stretch most of *us*.[23]

This enterprise—of living in Scripture and on the growing edge of the human situation in any given age— is a formidable, demanding task, not one for the faint-hearted or the slothful. But the true Wesleyan will settle for nothing less in a personal program for professional growth and development. It means living in the Scripture, not as a crossword puzzle for exegetes but as a font of insipiration and—yes, *revelation!* It means learning to think *biblically*. Furthermore, it means learning to live in the Christian past so that you can appropriate the lessons already learned by Christians in other times and circumstances, in their struggles for "a true gospel for *this* age" (whenever that "age" may have been). It means alertness and sensitivity to every new cultural development on the human horizon, without becoming "trendy" or falling easy prey to "every passing wind of doctrine" (cf. Eph. 4:14). It means profound reliance upon that inner nourishment of soul and mind that comes from the inner witness of the Holy Spirit—"no craven spirit but one that inspires us to strength, love and self-discipline" (as is well-said in 2 Timothy 1:17, NEB). Something like this is what is implied in taking Wesley (or Calvin or Augustine or Origen before him) as model or example. This is what is implied by our rich metaphor of "plundering the Egyptians."

Speaking practically, any such commitment involves an agenda of incessant reading, constant reflection, unquenchable curiosity, a restless quest for new perspectives, new alternatives to everything that is merely commonplace or to all reckless extremes on either side of each live issue. Remember that Wesley read as he rode, thought as he wrote, ruminated as he rested—that he was neither a harried man nor a self-pitying one. Thus, we can learn from him what it takes to combine a life of prayer and worship, of preaching and pastoral care, with a healthy curiosity about the world in which we minister. By precept and example, he could teach us what "inward" and "outward" holiness means: an outreach toward the perfecting of our love of God, plus a comparable love for all our neighbors that implies permanent social revolution. There are better and worse ways to implement this Wesleyan program—and we could usefully debate the alternatives in our own proposals for continuing education—alternatives seeking to translate our Wesleyan models into meaningful programs of our own. What matters for us is to realize that *something like this* belongs to the very essence of theologizing in the Wesleyan spirit: keeping our witness to Christ in active dialogue with this world in which he is to be proclaimed, this world for which he died. And if such a program is an "impossible possibility" (in Reinhold Niebuhr's famous phrase), then what more valid ideal could we ever set for ourselves? What less ought thoughtful laity ask of their pastors?

It is in some such spirit as this that I believe we can conceive of a truly Wesleyan way of doing theology nowadays—with open eyes to our heritage and our future, both within the wide, loving providence of God. These next three chapters are, therefore, offered as experiments (sketchy but serious) in recovering and updating the Wesleyan theology in this spirit, insofar as I see now how this might be done. My proposal, therefore, is to take Wesley's three central themes and to rehearse them in a way that I hope will be recognized as faithful to Wesley and yet also in an idiom that can be recognized as "contemporary." The ruling premise throughout is my conviction that every thoughtful Christian must accept responsibility for the overcoming of polarities without compromise, for affirming pluralism without drifting into indifferentism, for learning to live in the Scripture, the Christian past, and modern world all at once. And whatever its perplexities, we ought to think of any such project as an up reaching aspiration that will be sustained by the upholding grace of our Lord Jesus Christ, the unfailing love of God our Father, in the continuing communion and fellowship of his Holy Spirit.

In the midst of the Revival, Wesley took time out to try to describe this business of theology and culture ("plundering the Egyptians")—in what he meant to be a curriculum, or sorts, for continuing theological education. We may find it dated in some respects, yet I hope you will agree with me that it still has real relevance for us and for others like us. It is entitled *An Address to the Clergy* (1756)[24] and I offer you a test sampling from it as a way of confirming and concluding what I've been trying to say thus far. The well-furnished minister, says Wesley, must have "a capacity for reasoning with some closeness," "a lively turn of thought," "a good memory," "a competent share of knowledge." Then comes Scripture (in the original tongues), plus "a knowledge of history, . . . of sciences, . . . metaphysics, . . . natural philosophy, . . . the history of Christian thought and devotion, . . . a knowledge of the [contemporary] world. . . ." To knowledge and culture must be added "common sense, . . ." and "the animations of grace in one's affections and daily rounds": a clear sense of calling and a principled indifference to the blandishments of greed and ambition.

Brethren [says he in conclusion], is not this our calling . . .? And why (I will not say do we fall short, but why) are we satisfied with falling *so far* short of it? Is there any *necessity* laid upon us of sinking so infinitely below our calling? . . . Why then may not *you* be as "burning and shining lights" as those that have shone [before you]? Do you desire to partake of the same burning love, of the same shining holiness? Surely you do. You cannot but be sensible it is the greatest blessing which can be bestowed [on us]. . . . Then, as the Lord liveth, ye shall attain. . . . Then, assuredly, "the great Shepherd" of us and our flocks will "make *us* perfect in every good work to do his will, and work in us all that is well pleasing in his sight"! This is the desire and prayer of

Your Brother and Servant,
in our common Lord,
John Wesley

London, February 6, 1756.

2

DIAGNOSING THE HUMAN FLAW:
REFLECTIONS UPON
THE HUMAN CONDITION

ONE OF WESLEY'S AMBITIONS, never realized, was to bring all the English evangelicals, Church of England and Dissenters, into an active alliance. The Dissenters rejected him because of his Anglican loyalties; the Anglicans ostracized him because of his irregular churchmanship. Many in both camps argued that he had pared his list of Christian essentials too close to the bone. And it *was* a short list: "(1) original sin, (2) justification by faith alone, and (3) holiness of heart and life."[1] Here are the three central pillars of Wesleyan theology and I propose to re-present them, *seriatim*. Let us begin, therefore, with "original sin."

When was the last time you preached, or heard, a sermon on "original sin"? How many of you would take seriously the notion of a human flaw that is radical, inescapable, universal—a human malaise that cannot be cured or overcome by any of our self-help efforts or ethical virtues, however "moral" or aspiring—which is not, at the same time, of the actual essence of God's original design for the *humanum* (what he intended human existence to be)? How many of you are inclined to take seriously the old "articles" on "sin" in our various "confessions" and "articles of religion"? [2] Have you ever tried to reformulate this ancient doctrine in contemporary terms that conserve its valid intentions, supposing that you grant that its intentions are still valid? I still remember a lanky West Texas Pelagian in one of my first classes here who came by the office to complain that I *sounded* as if human sinning were something deeper and more mysterious than a failure of free will or a moral lapse. Such a strange idea intrigued him and he asked for suggestions for further reading. At the time, John Whale's *Christian Doctrine* was newly published, so I mentioned that. To his credit, he went off and found Whale, but was back again a fortnight later still more baffled— since Whale, as some of you know, was a good deal more of a "classical Protestant" on this point than I have ever been. We talked about it a while and finally he gave vent to a real outcry from his heart: "Well," said he, "if we don't have the power to *decide* to sin or *decide* not to sin, then all I've got to say is, 'God help us!'" This, of course, was an obvious cue for pointing out that he had unwittingly betrayed himself into involuntary orthodoxy!

For the crux of this whole ancient, vexed problem is

precisely the Pelagian contention that man is able to sin or not to sin as he chooses—so that if and when humans become aware that given acts are sinful, they are free, in their natural moral agency, to decide to go ahead ("for the hell of it") or else to inhibit their behavior. Here is the swirling vortex of centuries of controversy, and the passage between its two extremes is booby-trapped on both sides. For if you argue that we are sinful by nature (i.e., that the power only to sin is the actual human condition), you are also on the verge of saying that the original sin is simply being human—and that's heresy. If you take the opposite side, and argue that we *can* banish sin from our own lives and societies whenever we muster up sufficient moral effort (prodded inwardly by conscience and outwardly by moral example and admonition), you are on the verge of saying that sin is, in essence, a sort of social dysfunction, corrigible by moral insight and effort, or by proper programs of social reform. If you then persist in arguing for *original* sin, in some sense or other, you may be implying that we are sort of badly botched animals since, clearly, no other animal "sins" with anything like the same regularity, recklessness, and tragic consequence as does the human animal. But this is heresy as well—for it denies the moral uniqueness of the human creation.

Now, the obvious "gospel" for people able not to sin if they so will—to sin or not to sin, *that* is the question!—is salvation by moral rectitude. This, however stated, is in reality a gospel of *self*-salvation. According to this formula, it is self-understanding and self-direction that make up the recipe for human happiness. The gospel for the radically sinful, on the other hand, must say something about one's justification by God (which is to say, salvation) as a divine initiative to which we humans may respond. God in Christ, so this gospel goes, has taken the initiative in overcoming the ruptured relations between himself and his alienated children. On Lutheran grounds, for example, it runs something like this: "You (or some of you) are accepted by God because of Christ's merits, despite all your moral defects. Accept God's acceptance of you, indomitable concupiscence and all. This is what faith means: to accept God's sheer unmerited favor ["just as I am, without one plea"]. You will still be *simul justus et peccator*—justified before God and still a sinner all at the same time—but your being justified by grace is what really counts." Lutherans are careful to leave open the question as to why some people accept their acceptance while so many others apparently do not.

Properly instructed Calvinists start from the same premise—that sin is radical and that justification is by divine fiat. Then they proceed with quite different nuances in the development of their doctrines of the Christian life. Some sinners—utterly undeserving of God's mercy, utterly unable to save themselves—may, by God's free election, have the righteousness of Christ *imputed* to them and so come to be regarded as righteous by God for Christ's sake, having no righteousness of their own to plead. This notion of *election* ("predestination") has three concomitant notions in traditional Calvinist soteriology: (1) limited atonement (since it is clear that the mass of humanity is not elected, in point of fact); (2) irrestible grace (else God's free election could be nullified); and (3) final perseverance (since God's will cannot finally be thwarted). This is the famous TULIP[3] syndrome and can be seen in its starkest form in the so-called "Lambeth Articles" of 1595 (drafted by William Whitaker, opposed by Peter Baro—*before* the Arminian controversy and *long before* the Synod of Dort). These "articles" are worth "resurrecting" here, for while they cannot be familiar to many moderns, Wesley knew them well and had studied the issues in the long, bitter controversy that stretched from Cartwright and Hooker to his own day.[4]

1. God from eternity hath predestinated certain men unto life; certain men he hath reprobated.
2. The moving or efficient cause of predestination unto life is not the foresight of faith, or of perseverance, or of good works, . . . but only the good will and pleasure of God.
3. There is predetermined a certain number of the predestinate, which can neither be augmented nor diminished.
4. Those who are not predestinated to salvation shall be necessarily damned for their sins.
5. A true, living, and justifying faith, and a sanctifying by the Spirit of God is not extinguished, . . . it vanisheth not away in the elect, either finally or totally.
6. A man . . . who is endued with a justifying faith is certain, with the full assurance of faith, of the remission of his sins and of his everlasting salvation by Christ.
7. Saving grace is . . . not granted, is not communicated, to all men, by which they may be saved *if they will*.
8. No man can come unto Christ unless it shall be given unto him, and unless the Father shall draw him; and

all men are not drawn by the Father, that they may come to the Son.

9. It is not in the will or power of every one to be saved.[5]

This statement was approved in a conference in Lambeth Palace, subscribed by the Archbishop of Canterbury (Dr. Whitgift) and approved by the Archbishop of York (Dr. Hutton). They were then quietly nullified by "Good Queen Bess" under the urging of Bishop Bancroft of London. This was the high-water mark for the cause of "high" Calvinism in the Church of England and it played its part in Wesley's lifelong bias against predestination. But the trouble was that, by Wesley's time, the Calvinists had appropriated the label "evangelical" to themselves alone—so that justification by faith and the TULIP syndrome had come to be identified by most English Christians as mutual implicates. Most of the alternative positions had been lumped together under the label "Arminianism," and this was generally identified with the gospel of moral rectitude. We shall have to look more closely at Wesley's so-called "Arminianism" as we go along.

Now, any doctrine of sin and depravity as a diagnosis of the human condition is a paradox. Few will deny that there is a lot of sinning (or at the very least, deplorable behavior) in the world. But whether it is "original" or some sort of social dysfunction—the fruitage of unevolved animal residues or a distinctively *human* flaw—is a thorny question with no clear, neat answers (except the wrong ones!). Why *should* we sin unless we are driven to it by demons or neurosis? Why can't we point to a single fully human and humane society, somewhere on this planet—moral, just, peaceable? We have no difficulty in idealizing such a human possibility. Obviously, we have very impressive moral potentials. Most of us have consciences to enforce our ego and social ideals, up to a point. Is it true, then, as St. Paul claims, "that when I want to do the right, only the wrong is within my reach"? Is it true (as he goes on to add) that "in my inmost self I delight in the law of God, but I also perceive a different law in my bodily members, fighting against the law that my reason approves, making me a prisoner under the law . . . of sin"? [6] And if this is *not* true, how else will we account for the amplitude, universality and tragedy of our failures to attain to God's moral design for human happiness? Why is there so much of "man's inhumanity to man"? Our answers, whatever they may be, are the nucleus of our doctrines of original sin. This, in turn, will help to shape one's doctrine of justification (by faith *or* good works). *That,* in turn, will affect all one's notions of the Christian life: how it is entered, how Christians mature, what our Christian hopes may be— here and hereafter. This, then, will direct our vision of "salvation"—i.e., the terms of human fulfillment and human happiness. This question about sin ("original" sin at that) is not, therefore, just an abstract speculation. It plagues *us* as agonizingly as it did Wesley. Something *has* gone fearfully awry in the human enterprise. Everywhere (and in our own hearts!) we see the signs of this tragic discrepancy between our visions of what human existence ought to be and what it actually ever is. But what is the human potential—and why do we fall short of it, all of us, one way or another? No one can live responsibly or help others to live responsibly without thoughtful answers to these questions—*now!*

How John Wesley came to his own mature doctrine of the human flaw—and to a gospel that could match it— is a complicated story that I have only recently begun to think I can sort out (since the conventional accounts of it have never seemed quite credible). He says, more than once, that the doctrine of justification by faith alone was a novelty to him before 1738, and to many others in the Church of England as well.[7] This cannot have been literally true, for he could not have studied theology in Oxford from 1720 to 1735 without becoming aware of the famous controversy on this very point (Downham and Davenant *vs.* Taylor and Hammond, John Bunyan *vs.* Richard Baxter, *et al.*),[8] to say nothing of the official statements in the Thirty-Nine Articles and the Homilies to which he had subscribed. What he meant was that he had grown up with the gospel of moral rectitude, and that this was the dominant view in Anglican soteriology as he knew it. The premise of such a gospel was the human moral ability to sin only by choice. Its prescription for the Christian life, therefore, was moral effort, encouraged, sanctioned, and rewarded by the church (through her "means of grace"). It included the doctrines of baptismal regeneration and a sacramental life that, in some sense, guaranteed grace. His early sermons[9] —together with his very interesting theological discussions with his mother (his first and best theological tutor)—all reflect an earnest dedication of his life and labors to the high goals of holy living, holy dying and of

Christian happiness in God, not the world. Two of its manuals (favorites in the Epworth rectory) were Lorenzo Scupoli's *Spiritual Struggle*[10] and Henry Scougal's *The Life of God in the Soul of Man*.[11] It is not only unfair, but misleading, to depreciate the Christian intentions enshrined in this gospel of moral rectitude. The Methodist stereotypes of irreligious Anglican parsons have their grain of truth but are obviously also self-serving (to inflate Methodist egos) ; they ignore the spiritual achievements of eighteenth century Anglicanism. The *real* problem with this doctrine of a moral ability not to sin except at will (for Wesley and for all its other adherents then and ever since) was the tragic discrepancy between its promises and performance. For all his zeal and devotion—in Oxford and Epworth and Georgia—he never found the happiness or the serenity that the holy living tradition advertised. The Holy Club was not "a happy club." The refugee missionary from Georgia was a miserable victim of his own frustrated ideals.

Even so, the alternative offered him by the Moravians and Salzburgers in Georgia and, later, by Peter Böhler in England was hard to take—and this is what made Aldersgate so dramatic an event that it has overshadowed the larger theological mutation that took place *throughout* the year 1738 (beginning with his shipboard memorandum of Tuesday, January 24th,[12] through the formation of the Religious Society at Fetter Lane on May 1st,[13] Aldersgate itself,[14] the visit to Germany, June 14th to September 16th,[15] Wesley's discovery of Jonathan Edwards's *Faithful Narrative* on October 9th,[16] and finally, his production of *The Doctrine of Salvation, Faith and*

Good Works, Extracted from the Homilies of the Church of England [November 12th]).[17] What really matters is that, by that year's end, he had made a decisive switch from the gospel of moral rectitude to "justification by faith alone" *(sola fide)*—i.e., to a doctrine of a radical, universal human flaw—from all talk about human merit to radical trust in God's pardon as a *gift,* in and through the merits of Christ's mediatorial sacrifice. The Aldersgate story in the *Journal* is very carefully reconstructed so as to focus the convergence of two great Christian traditions that had been in painful tension ("holy living" and faith alone) upon one single "moment" in a single place, after two centuries of conflict. This is why its climax is so readily misconstrued when isolated from the account as a whole. How many of us have traced out Wesley's careful *background* analysis of his heartwarming? Or, again, how many have pondered that later *Journal* entry of January 4, 1739, where he says of himself: "But that I am not a Christian *at this day* [seven months *after* Aldersgate] I as assuredly know as that Jesus is the Christ."[18]

The essence of the Aldersgate experience was a sudden new assurance that "I did trust in Christ, Christ alone, for salvation . . . that Christ had taken away my sins, even mine, and had saved me from the law of sin and death." This was Wesley's personal appropriation of the classical Protestant diagnosis of the human plight along with the classical Protestant gospel of "faith alone," *sola fide.* Its presupposition was a stress on the human flaw as radical (incurable by any human effort or merit). *This* was the sense in which Wesley could claim (as he did) that, on the point of justification by faith alone, he stood no more than a hair's breadth from Calvin—or any other true "evangelical."[19]

Real trouble began—and here's where the plot of Wesleyan theologizing really begins to thicken!—when he balked at going further and accepting the entire Protestant package. The first breach was with the Moravians and their Lutheran doctrine of invincible concupiscence. Then, *vis-à-vis* the Calvinists, he rejected the last four of their "five points." This was less a deliberate decision than an intractable bias against election, irresistible grace and final perseverance—because of what he took to be their moral (i.e., antinomian) implications. On the other side, his all-out advocacy of original sin and justification by faith alone had the effect of cutting him off from most of his Anglican contemporaries. His instinctive rejection of quietism wore out his earlier welcome with the Moravians. This helps to explain why the Wesleyan revival was so nearly a one-man operation and why no latitudinarians and very few "evangelical" Anglicans would cooperate with him or support his segment of the movement. The Dissenters wanted no part of his commitment to the Church of England as a comprehensive sacramental community. The resultant "third alternative" was an interesting and original—anomaly (viz., a Protestant doctrine of original sin minus most of the other elements in classical Protestant soteriology, *plus* a catholic doctrine of perfection *without* its full panoply of priesthood and priestcraft).[20] Thus, he stood exposed to charges of inconsistency from both sides. Even after justification by faith alone had become his central message, he retained the holy living tradition of his upbringing and he taught his people not only to go on toward perfection but to "expect to be made perfect in love in this life"! This caught him in a crossfire—a catholic who had become an evangelical and yet never ceased to be catholic: i.e., an evangelical-catholic! This was an ecumenical move of prime importance—and could be even more relevant today than then, because now it just might be more fully appreciated by more people, if it were really understood (and if we could ever get Wesley rescued from his too-exclusive Methodist identification and recognized for the ecumenical theologian that he was and meant to be).

The critical nuance here is the difference in his doctrine of "original sin" and "total depravity" from what Gilbert Rowe taught me to call "*tee*-total depravity" (i.e., the Lutheran and Calvinist diagnoses of the human condition). The twofold clue here is in (1) Wesley's (essentially catholic) view of sin as a malignant *disease* rather than an obliteration of the *imago Dei* in fallen human nature, and (2) in his displacement of the doctrine of "election" with the notion of "prevenient grace." He could have gotten his particular doctrine of prevenience from Bellarmine, for he is closer to Bellarmine *on this point* than to Calvin—and we know that he had read Bellarmine's *De Justificatione* and the history of the Roman Catholic controversy over grace and free will between the Jesuits and Dominicans. But a more obvious source for "prevenience," in this sense, was his own Anglican tradition.[21] In any case, this is one of the "new" questions that Roman Catholics and Anglicans and Methodists ought to explore together, with a few Lutherans and Calvinists thrown into the mix to keep everybody honest. The old chasms between Protestants and Catholics on sin and free will, and on justification and grace, have altered their form and substance in the past two decades or so, and it would be fruitful for Wesley's ideas about sin and grace to be included in any serious reconsideration of the problem at this new stage of the dialogue.

His driving passion was to find a third alternative to Pelagian optimism and Augustinian pessimism with respect to the human flaw and the human potential. In his early gospel of moral rectitude, original sin (as an entail of Adam's fall) was washed away in baptismal regeneration, leaving behind a "tinderbox of sin" (the *fomes peccati*) together with a residual moral ability to sin or not sin, as one might choose. And if one chose to sin, one could still repent, bring forth fruits meet for repentance and be assured of God's pardon, by the church (on the basis of her "power of the keys"). The crucial aim in this tradition was to hold persons responsible for their deeds and misdeeds, and to stifle amoralisms of every kind. Its proposed remedy for the human flaw (and Wesley's, too, before 1738) was dual: (1) earnest moral effort, guided by the church; and (2) faithful use of the means of grace which the church alone supplies. This optimism, of course, was undercut by any truly *radical* doctrine of sin, as one can realize from the Duchess of Buckingham's toplofty complaint to the Countess of Huntingdon (an evangelical blue blood all the way!):

I thank your ladyship for the information concerning the Methodist preachers. Their doctrines are most repulsive and strongly tinctured with impertinence and disrespect towards their superiors, in perpetually endeavouring to level all ranks and do away with all distinctions. It is monstrous to be told that you have a heart as sinful as the common wretches that crawl the earth.[22]

A somewhat more substantial denial of all notions of sin as radical came from Dr. John Taylor of Norwich. In a famous book in 1740, he argued that men do sin (obviously!), but they *could* do otherwise, and they should be guided and admonished to do so. "They can do their duty *if* they choose!" Taylor's blithe confidence in human autonomy struck Wesley as profoundly unbiblical and anti-evangelical—and he reacted quickly with the longest piece he ever wrote: *The Doctrine of Original Sin, According to Scripture, Reason and Experience.*[23] Then, in 1759, he digested "Part I" of the treatise into a sermon that was then placed first in volume IV of the *Sermons* (1760). In both treatise and sermon, Wesley takes the Protestant hard line, asserting the utter impotence of man's *natural* moral powers. Fallen man was (and is) "by *nature* purely evil . . . unmixed with anything of an opposite nature. . . . He never deviated into good"!

In our naturally sinful condition, we "have no more significant knowledge of God than the beasts of the field. . . . Having no proper knowledge of God we have no love of him. . . . Every man born into the world is a rank idolater. . . . We have set up our idols in our hearts, . . . we worship ourselves. . . . We seek happiness in the creature, instead of the Creator." This doctrine, he goes on to insist, "is the first distinguishing point between heathenism and Christianity." In pagan morality (and in natural morality) the presupposition is that "the natural good much overbalances the evil. Christianity [on the other hand] makes sin a shibboleth: 'Is man by nature filled with all manner of evil? Is he void of all good? Is he wholly fallen? Is his soul totally corrupted?' . . . Allow this and you are so far a Christian. Deny it and you are but a heathen still."

This is a grim picture and verges on the Augustinian-Calvinist extreme. And yet (and there's always a "not-yet" whenever Wesley tilts toward any extreme), he immediately yokes the doctrine of total depravity with its antidote (where "total" means that *all* of the *humanum* is "depraved," rather than that none of it is anything but depraved): (1) God's own *therapeia psychēs* (his *curative* activity within our hearts) and (2) God's universally active initiative in calling sinners to authentic repentance and self-knowledge. This is pre-venient and here is where "prevenient" grace functions as an alternative to *election*. Sin is spoken of as a sickness that can be cured by the Great Physician if we will accept his threefold prescription: (1) repentance (self-knowledge), (2) renunciation of self-will, and (3) faith (trust in God's sheer, unmerited grace). "The great end of religion is to renew our hearts in the image of God, to repair that total loss of righteousness and true holiness which we sustained by the sin of our first parents." [24]

What is original here is Wesley's stout upholding of the sovereignty of grace but not its irresistibility—and this distinction deserves more pondering than it usually gets. Sinners can do literally nothing to save themselves (not by merit, nor demerit, nor by the will to believe). And yet God's intention in creating persons (which gives each person his/her unique identity) is not thwarted by human resistance, because it is God's own purpose that the offer of grace shall be experienced *as optional*. The chief function of prevenient grace, therefore, is to stir the sinner to repentance (which is to say, to a valid self-understanding of his/her sinfulness). Thus, Wesley can speak of repentance as the *porch* of religion, of faith as the *door,* and of holiness as religion itself.[25]

What happens in repentance is a sort of self-recognition that identifies spiritual pride and self-righteousness and rejects them both as inauthentic. This allows us to realize that it is God, for Christ's sake, who can and who has forgiven all our sins and broken the power of sin and death in our hearts. Thus, it is repentance that also calls us to faith and to that trust in God that alters the basis of our existence.

It is just here that Wesley takes a turn away from the classical Protestant soteriology. Luther and Calvin regarded the residue of sin *(fomes peccati)* not only as ineradicable but sinful as such; it falls under God's righteous condemnation even though this does not forfeit his justifying grace. Wesley distinguishes between "sin properly so-called" (i.e., a conscious, deliberate violation of a known law of God) and *involuntary* sins and misdeeds. This, obviously, presupposes that residual sin *(fomes peccati)* diminishes in force and influence as the Christian grows in grace. There *are* "wandering thoughts," [26] and these must be sent packing. There is "sin in believers" [27] and this must be repented of, promptly. "Sin *remains* but no longer *reigns*." [28] Those who are justified by faith alone are led, by the Holy Spirit in their consciences, to discover "new" sins, or their sinful abuses of innocent human aspirations— and to recognize temptations which, if entertained seriously enough to form moral intentions, will result in the forfeiture of one's justification.[29] This notion of the Christian way as forever perilous offended the Calvinists' reliance upon "final perseverance." It seemed to them as if Wesley's God was unable to keep his own elect unto the day of their salvation. For Wesley, however, it was just this double notion of sin as reducible and of faith as a risky business that reinforced his stress on Christian self-discipline (moral *and* spiritual). For as the believer learns to repent daily, and to trust God's grace, and to grow in that grace, then he begins to move from the threshold of faith (justification) toward its fullness (sanctification). This particular linkage between *sola fide* (justification) and "holy living" (sanctification) has no precedent, to my knowledge, anywhere in classical Protestantism.

For our purposes in updating the Wesleyan tradition for these times a good deal of Wesley's rhetoric and conceptual apparatus may safely be left back there with the rest of his eighteenth century culture. Literal notions of Adam's fall or of the seminal transmission of sin and guilt are unintelligible to the modern mind, even when it tries to think biblically. The essence of human sin is not the helpless repetition of Adam's act—even though there *is* an analogue here for understanding how insatiable our human hungers for a knowledge of good and evil really are. Sin is not our actual misdeeds, nor even the evil impulses that still lurk in the murky depths of the human heart. Sin, in its essence, is human *overreach*—the reckless abuse of our distinctive human outreachings and upreachings—those aspirations that make us human but whose corruptions make us less than truly human. Sin is the bitter fruit of pride. It springs from our intimations of the infinite and our desires to avoid or escape the actual terms of our finite existence. Sin is our unwillingness to be radically dependent upon God "for life and breath and all things." It is, therefore, the idolatry of preferring to be "gods" rather than truly human (which was, of course, the primal temptation in Eden).

The fruit of sin is *bondage* (i.e., slavery to our own self-deceptions, to our illusions about life and society that stir up utopias that never quite transpire). The result of our overreaching in each of our distinctively human out-reaches does not bring the real self-satisfaction that we keep on expecting, but rather tragic self-stultification instead (and for this there is no fully rational or even morally acceptable explanation—since our self-excuses do not finally satisfy).

For example, an overreaching aspiration to freedom, if successful, presently tempts one to the *abuse* of his freedom and to a denial of that freedom to others. Groups that achieve liberation slide almost unwittingly into oppressions of their own. Overreaching intelligence turns into intellectual arrogance. Overreaching aspirations to self-knowledge and self-control turn into narcissism and self-deception. Joy that is snatched at, or clung to, is tainted by transience, and brings on nostalgia or depression—or else to redoubled efforts to be happy, none of them with anything approaching lasting satisfaction. Human love is forever overreaching itself—it is incontinent by nature (that is its glory and misery). It never willingly comes to terms with the brackets of finitude, symbolized most harshly by death. This is "human bondage."

In the Old Testament, the phrase "house of bondage" connotes both Egyptian slavery and also the sinful state of humanity.[30] Paul uses the phrase "the spirit of bondage" as a synonym for sin.[31] The human flaw and this spirit of bondage are, in this sense, paired metaphors for the human abuse of the human potential for creative freedom *and* also the tragic consequences of such abuses in the frail textures of a humane society.

But there is no *necessity* for this, no divine purpose that compels such creatures as we were meant to be to have become the creatures that we are. There is no *good* reason why human outreach *has* to overreach itself. Sin and sinners cannot, therefore, justify or excuse themselves. *This* is "the mystery of iniquity"[32] which we need to ponder alongside "the mystery of godliness."[33] If the human flaw inheres in our merely being human, then every promise of salvation is some sort of legal fiction which will never satisfy our hunger for true and full humanity. If, on the other hand, sin is merely social dysfunction, then it ought in principle to be corrigible and salvation ought really to be possible by some formula or program of self-salvation or group-salvation. And yet in the long history of social activism there is no evidence whatever that persons or groups or societies have ever achieved their full human potential by means of human wisdom or heroism or even "letting be" (save on some relative scale of amelioration that always falls short of our proper human hunger for the utmost). Nor is there any credible prospect for it, apart from the euphoric visions of our currently fashionable "human potential" optimists.

Our real dilemma lies deeper—in this tragic welter of aspirations that corrupt each other. "O, wretched man that I am" (Rom. 7:24)—even if I have learned the newly sacrosanct Pelagian litany, "I'm O.K., You're O.K.!" The fact of the human tragedy is everywhere and inescapable—in lives whose humanity is denied or despoiled by others, in lives that reach out for happiness and yet are mocked by disappointment, doomed to death. Who or what could possibly deliver us from this primordial tragedy without robbing us of our freedom and thus also of our full humanity? The only answer I can think of (or have ever heard of), not already clearly falsified in human experience itself over the decades and centuries, is some sort of active intervention in our lives and in our human history by that purpose and power of whatever or whoever it was that ever intended us to be free and joyous and loving to begin with.

Is there such a power or purpose or person? Is there any such intention that is in fact our human destiny? Whatever we have to say to questions like these had better contain all the clues in our faith and all the insights that have turned up in our efforts to help God's prodigal sons and daughters find their way back home to the Father's house. Wesley had some thoughts on this, too, as one might expect, and those thoughts and their possible relevance for our efforts to understand and communicate the gospel, will furnish us with grist for further comment.

3

ON "OFFERING CHRIST"
THE GIST OF THE GOSPEL

WE HAVE BEEN SPEAKING OF THE HUMAN FLAW, and of its bitter fruit in human bondage. But is there an honest answer to the anguished question, "Who shall deliver us *from* this bondage?" Wesley thought there was. His whole career was an astonishing demonstration of a gospel that effected a Christian revolution in his time and society, and for a full century afterwards. In a hundred different ways on thousands of different occasions, decade after five decades his one consistent message was Jesus Christ and him crucified— *Christus crucifixus, Christus redemptor, Christus victor.* First Corinthians 1:30 was one of his favorite texts (72 times altogether) and, as we noted above, his favorite single text during the first crucial half-year of the Revival.[1]

45

For example, on July 17th of that year, he came to Bath where he fell into a casual disputation with a gentleman who remembered his Oxford reputation for being "a little crack-brained." "However [Wesley goes on] some persons who were not of his mind, having pitched on a convenient place . . . on top of the hill under which the town lies, I there *offered Christ* to about a thousand people for 'wisdom, righteousness, sanctification and redemption' [1 Cor. 1:30]. Thence I returned to Bath and preached on 'What must I do to be saved?' [Acts 16:30*b*] to a larger audience than ever before."[2]

The burden of his evangelical message was always the same; the references are almost monotonous. He speaks of "preaching Christ," of "offering Christ," "proclaiming Christ," "declaring Christ," [3] and so forth. And always it was the gospel of salvation by grace through faith, justification and deliverance through God's grace in Christ. It was a projection—across half a century and three kingdoms—of his discovery at Aldersgate, his unwavering conviction that the essence of authentic Christian experience is trusting Christ, Christ alone, for salvation, a trust that generates an inward "assurance . . . that Christ has taken away *my* sins, even *mine*, and has saved *me* from the law of sin and death."[4]

Time was, as we know, when *evangelical* and *evangelism* were dirty words for liberals in general—and this included, as a matter of course, the majority of the Methodists (at least the clergy). We thought we had outgrown nineteenth century revivalism and the sort of private piety that clings to Jesus and ignores the human agonies of this world, this world for which Christ died.

To this day, there is a sort of litmus-paper test of a person's theological reactions and type. If you can hear (or sing)

> Jesus paid it all,
> All to him I owe,
> Sin had left a crimson stain,
> He washed it white as snow,

with serious meaning and without queasiness, you're either not as liberal as you thought or else somebody has been tampering with your liberalism. Either way, the test will serve as an indication that the whole problem of justification by faith alone is still in unresolved confusion in the minds and hearts of many Methodists—those, that is, who allow themselves to *ponder* their faith and its problems.

Nowadays however, and almost suddenly, "evangelism" has become a bandwagon "trend"—with all sorts of different groups eager to be aboard. Self-styled evangelicals are speaking up for social action; social activists are claiming that their concerns (and agenda) are evangelistic, too (whoever thought otherwise?). The World Council of Churches has had a "conference" on it (with another planned), we now have the "Lausanne Covenant," The United Methodist Church's Council of Bishops is considering a major declaration on evangelism, and the Roman Catholics have asked that it be included in the agenda of their continuing consultations with the Methodists. I'm as eager and delighted as anybody else about this new enthusiasm and its opening horizons. I even remember an old story of Hal Luccock's, explaining how Catholics and Episcopalians had crosses on their steeples as symbols of their faith in Christ crucified, how Congregationalists had weather vanes up there as tokens of their democratic convictions, whereas Methodists usually had lightning rods, in memory of having once been struck and their fear lest it happen again!

Even so, much of our talk about evangelism remains confused and in need of a careful theological sorting-out. I do not pretend, of course, to be able to do this for The United Methodist Church at large, but I've learned enough from Wesley by now to realize that the issues involved in "offering Christ" to the masses were not at all simple; that he was trying to find and hold to the way between the pitfalls of pietism and antinomianism on one side of the truth and of moralism and works-righteousness on the other side. Unless you're reckless with your words, "evangelical" denotes (and always has denoted) *salvation by faith in Christ crucified,* salvation as the gift of God's unmerited grace, provided freely in and through Christ's suffering love, with no prior moral achievement or merit from the human side. Since the fifth century, "evangelical" has been an antonym to Pelagian moralism in any of its protean forms. But what of the new secular pieties and the new antinomianisms that are now flourishing in our midst?

Most of us know the climactic passage in Tillich's most famous sermon, "You Are Accepted." It has been quoted by Alan Walker in his latest book, which gives it some sort of evangelical *nihil obstat.* And, certainly, it is a valid and eloquent distillate of an essential element in "pure" Lutheran orthodoxy:

You are accepted. You are *accepted,* accepted by that which is greater than you. Do not ask for its name now: perhaps you will find it later. Do not try to do *anything* now; perhaps later you will do much. Do not seek for anything; do not perform anything; do not intend anything. *Simply accept the fact that you are accepted.*[5]

What is missing here, of course, is any approximation to the Lutheran Christology (there is no mention of Christ anywhere in the sermon). Nor is there any emphasis whatever on those "good works following *after* faith" that orthodox Lutherans have always stressed. But the instant popularity of this gospel of unconditional acceptance was a sign of that deep relief most moderns feel when anybody offers to cancel all moral conditions for their acceptability—either in relation to God *or vis-à-vis* their fellow human beings. It is heartwarming to think that one is accepted, no matter what; this, of course, is the grain of truth in *I'm O.K., You're O.K.*—just as I am, because *I am.* There is a new egalitarianism in our midst and one bucks a strong tide whenever one wonders aloud about credentials, or standards, or the criteria of one's acceptability (moral, academic, or in any other sphere).

Now it is the antinomianism implied in this classical Protestant version of justification as God's acceptance of the sinner in his sin, *no matter what,* that Romans and Anglicans have always feared in the traditional Protestant soteriology, because they see it allowing (yea, encouraging) a pious disregard of moral rules and codes in favor of personal spontaneity in freedom and love (i.e., situation ethics). There is, of course, a world of difference between Luther's doctrine of justification and Tillich's (not their only difference, either, as you may know). Luther faced the manifest scandals of medieval moralism and sacerdotalism and tried to rescue the gospel of God's *unmerited* mercy from their doctrines of merit correlated with their sacerdotal dispensations and disciplines. Tillich had *memories* of a conventional morality of discipline and repression, but he himself had long been liberated from any such traditions by the new amoralisms of the German intelligentsia of the 1920s to which he belonged.[6] Moreover, Luther's stress on Scripture and its Christocentric emphases has no counterpart in Tillich nor the standard Lutheran disjunction between soteriology and culture.

The point to all this for our purposes is that Wesley's heart was strangely warmed "as one was reading *Luther's* preface to the Epistle to the Romans" (May 24, 1738). Later (June 15, 1741), when he finally got around to a more careful reading of Luther's *Commentary on Galatians*, he reacted negatively[7] to what he regarded as its implicit irrationalism and antinomianism. Thus it was that with respect to the relationships between law and gospel and also the specific mode of Christ's redemptive work, Wesley was closer to Calvin than to Luther. But then, after 1765 or thereabouts, under increasing pressure from the "imputationists," Wesley began to pull away from the Calvinists, too, and returned, more and more, to his native holy-living tradition (without, however, abandoning the *sola fide*).[8] From 1770 until his death, the breach with the Calvinists was open and bitter. They never forgave Wesley his synergism; he never dropped his charge that their predestination theories were a charter for antinomianism.

The ruling metaphor of classical Protestant soteriology has always been the courtroom, together with a cluster of forensic concepts about a human offender arraigned before the divine judge who must, if justice is not to be mocked, convict and condemn the offender. What happens then, in the case of the elect, however, is a juridical move in which the judge decides (or has already decided) to commute the sinner's sentence, on the basis of the imputed righteousness of *Christ*. This becomes the *formal* cause of one's justification, whereby the sinner acquires Christ's own perfect righteousness as the just ground for his/her own *acquittal* by God from all condemnation. This is what justification means: to be pardoned, to be regarded and treated as righteous, in and through Christ's saving merit. This forensic imagery has its roots in the Bible (although it is not at all dominant there). It had flourished in feudalism (it is, for example, the presupposition of Anselm's theory of substitutionary atonement [9]). Thereafter, it had been radically transformed in the Reformation, largely by the wiping out of the priestly apparatus that had grown up around it.

There is (we might mention in passing, almost marginally) a very tangled lexical problem here with regard to the biblical terms in which these crucial issues have been defined.[10] The Greek word *dikaioō* belongs to a class of verbs that are formed from adjectives: e.g., *typhlos* = blind; *typhloō* = to blind—*psychros* = cool; *psychroō* = to cool. *Dikaios* means "just"; *dikaioō* means to make just (to strengthen in virtue) or, alternatively, to declare just (as in a court's verdict of acquittal). But this is ambiguous: you can *declare* a person to be "not guilty" ("just" in that sense) but you cannot *make* a person righteous or "just" by *doing* something to that person. Thus, most Pauline exegetes agree that *dikaioō* is used by St. Paul forensically. And yet when divine action is involved, there must be more than a mere juridical acquittal. "Righteousness" may be *imputed* to a person and he/she may thereby be justified before God, through the merits of Christ. But is nothing like actual righteousness *imparted* at the same time? What is meant by the promise that "if a man is in Christ, he is a new creature . . ."? Does this not imply an actual change of character, along with the change in the God-human relationship? Wesley thought so and was, therefore, committed to a doctrine of justification that involved both a relative and a real change in the forgiven sinner (a relative change in one's forensic status before God and a real change in the moral quality of one's interpersonal relationships).

The official doctrines of the Church of England reflect this forensic tradition (especially in the XXXIX Articles) but Anglicanism had also retained a *therapeutic* emphasis as well: justification as a healing, restorative act, as the turning point in the course of a malignant disease, the beginning of a convalescent process, the goal of which is the complete restoration of the corrupted image of God in man. Justification, then, in Hooker and Taylor and Wesley is both acquittal *and* renewal, imputation *and* impartation, a relative and yet also a real

change. In the forensic model of justification, the meaning of 1 Corinthians 5:19 had been reversed, as if
St. Paul had said that "God was in Christ reconciling
himself to the world . . ." (one can even see this in
the Anglican Articles, as in No. II). Wesley did not
change this part of the Articles and it still appears in
our former Methodist Articles, also No. II. Happily, in
Article VIII of the former Evangelical United Brethren
"Confession," we find the original Pauline form, "God
was in Christ reconciling the world to himself"—which
means that, somewhat absent-mindedly, United Methodists
have it *both* ways!

By Wesley's time, this older forensic tradition had
been generally displaced by what I've been labelling
"the gospel of moral rectitude." Thus, he grew up in an
Anglican rectory, got his education in an Anglican
school and university and then served the Church of
England as priest and missionary for more than a decade,
with no personal conviction as to salvation by imputation. It is not true, of course, as our typical Methodist
hagiography has it, that the young Wesley and his
contemporaries (by and large) were mere moralists.
When, at the Lord's Table, they prayed (more often
than *we* do), "We do not presume to come to this, thy
Table, trusting in our own righteousness but in thy
manifold and great mercy, We are not worthy . . . but
thou art the same Lord whose property is always to have
mercy," their intentions were as solifidian as any Lutheran's or Calvinist's ever was. But they did insist on a
synergism of grace in the sequence of repentance, faith
and good works—which is why Wesley never repudiated

his one great pre-Aldersgate sermon, "The Circumcision of the Heart," with its holy-living theme and its reversed order of placing holiness (in the nascent form of congruent merit) *before* justification. Indeed, he included it in his forty-four "standard sermons"—out of its chronological order!

Even so, it is a fact—it is the *central* fact in the Wesleyan Revival—that from 1738 onwards, Wesley taught the *sola fide* as the first and last article by which the church (and with it the gospel) stands or falls. And yet, he sought a third alternative even here: a fusion of imputation *and* impartation that included both Protestant and catholic emphases and that brought him reproaches from Anglicans and Calvinists alike. But I have come to believe that it is just this third alternative that has become more and more relevant for ecumenical theology today—especially when all the old forensic images in morality and religion are fading fast or have already lost their decisive influence. Wesley's evangelistic message *combines* radical faith in God's reconciling love in Christ (the inward, personal dimension of salvation) *with* a moral and social agenda implied in and by this love that energizes and guides the Christian life from new birth to maturation, always "in Christ."

We may take two of Wesley's most famous sermons as a summary of this "offering of Christ": (1) "Justification by Faith" (1746)[11] and (2) "The Scripture Way of Salvation" (1765).[12] In "Justification by Faith," there are four questions asked and answered.

Question one: Why and wherefore *justification?* Answer: *Sin*—and here we have Wesley's doctrine of original sin recapitulated in striking, pungent fashion. Until the sinner is *justified,* his radical unrighteousness leaves him open to a richly deserved unhappiness and damnation.

Question two: What *is* justification? The answer here is threefold: (a) it is *not* sanctification; (b) it is *not* bare acquittal, least of all an acquittal in which God "believes us righteous when we are unrighteous"; [13] (c) it *is* "pardon, the forgiveness of sins." [14]

Question three: "Who are they that are justified?" Answer: The ungodly. Here, however, Wesley turns his own "holy living" tradition around and produces something original. We have seen how that tradition had placed holy intentions ahead of justification. This was the notion that some sort of outward evidence of one's spiritual aspirations ("good works") is prerequisite to actual justification. In 1738, and thereafter, Wesley reversed this order by 180 degrees. "All truly good works *follow* after justification"; justification is, therefore, only for those who have no merit of their own. "Just as I am, without one plea . . ." *is* an authentic evangelical sentiment.

Wesley has a fourth question: On what *terms* may the ungodly be justified? The answer here is *faith,* with no necessary conditions of antecedent obedience of the moral law. And what is faith? It is not only a *belief* in God in Christ (this is mere orthodoxy and the devils are orthodox). It is, rather, "a sure trust and confidence that Christ died for my *sins,* that he loved *me,* and gave himself for *me,*" etc. Faith is the *necessary* condition of justification, and the only *necessary* one (hence "faith alone," *sola fide*). Whatever else we may bring to God, of virtue and holy intentions, repentance and good works, none is a *necessary* condition. Wesley's aim here is to wipe out all possible human pride or complacency in one's salvation and to establish "Jesus [Christ] as the whole and sole propitiation for our sins."

"The Scripture Way of Salvation" is a maturer formulation of Wesley's "offering of Christ," made necessary, in Wesley's judgment, by twenty years of further development in the ferments of the Revival. In this sermon the central questions are reduced to three: What is salvation? What is saving faith? How are we saved *by* faith? Wesley's answers are basically the same as before, but much has been gained in the interim by way of altered nuance, in reaction to misunderstandings among both followers and critics. To begin with, he stresses prevenient grace (which is resistible), and argues that this is a better explanation of the divine initiative than predestination and irresistible grace. He repeats his aphorism that "justification is another word for *pardon*," and then moves on to the controverted issue of the interrelations between justification and sanctification. He denies that these two are different aspects of a single event, and he carefully places sanctification *after* justification, in the ontological order of salvation. They are, however, concurrent in time. When and as we are forgiven, we are also born again, and on the very same terms: i.e., the merits of Christ's atoning love. Thus Wesley can speak of a *relative* change in our status before God (justification), which is all the Moravians and the Puritans would allow in *any* case. But he insists on adding an equal emphasis on the *real* change that takes place in our hearts, lives, and loves—as we become "new creatures in Christ." Thus, he is able to interpret salvation as a *process:* one that begins with justification but that continues thereafter as the regenerate person grows in grace toward sanctification as a flying goal. Justification is what God does *for* us; sanctification is what God does *in* us. In justification we *gain* God's favor; holy-living is the life-process in which we seek to *retain* it (a distinction that runs back to Philip Melanchthon!). Justification is the *threshold* of faith; sanctification its *fullness.*

This life-process is by no means placid nor is its triumphant eventuation ever guaranteed, which is, of course, yet another rejection of any notion of final perseverance. The Christian does not commit *willful* sin. If he does, he loses God's favor and backslides into condemnation. But the impulse and power of sin are not *"destroyed"* in justification or regeneration. They are only "suspended." "Wandering thoughts" (the *fomes peccati)* remain, and these must be dealt with in terms of daily repentance, daily renewals of faith, daily exercises of love.

Thus, Wesley understood justification as God's work *for* the repentant sinner, with Christ's mediatorial sacrifice as its sole meritorious cause—to which our only proper response is "acceptance" (i.e., faith). But in the very same transaction there is also a work of divine grace *in* the sinner's heart and moral disposition. Wesley calls this "regeneration" or "new birth," the beginning of the actual restoration of the *imago Dei*, the impartation, by grace, of our "original justice": our God-given power to love God above all else and all else in God. Justification and regeneration are two aspects of the same mysterious outpouring or inflooding of grace. It is ambiguous and confusing if we blur this distinction between God's action *for* the sinner (reconciliation in love) and God's action *in* the pardoned sinner's heart (restoration of moral responsibility of the human power to avoid or desist from intentional sin). We have no part in our own justification before God, save the passive act of accepting and trusting the merits of Christ. But we do have a crucial part to play in the further business of "growing up into Christ, unto the stature of the perfect man." You can almost always identify a "fundamentalist" theology by noticing, in its preoccupation with soteriology, an indifference to human responsibility in the consequent struggle for God's righteous rule in *all* of human life and society. Conversely, you can find liberalism's cachet in its concern for the Christian's moral and social agenda, with a relative indifference to the fundament on which that agenda rightly rests. The liberal speaks easily of Christ as revealer and exemplar but tends to stammer when pressed back toward any evangelical notions of mediatorial sacrifice. This is why neither fundamentalists nor liberals have a more than tenuous hold on the *full* Christian tradition, as we have seen Wesley trying to put it together and hold it together. Methodists, in his train, have a less than impressive record in doing this as well as he did.

Wesley's first point is that, before and apart from justification, we have only the power to sin even when we "try" not to—and, obviously, we are busy in our exercise of this tragic power. Justification is God's acceptance of just such a sinful person, on account of Christ's merits. Our part in the transaction is a faithful, grateful acceptance of God's acceptance of us. Regeneration is also a work of grace, and with it come the bare beginnings of a restored power to avoid or desist from "known sins." This opens up the possibility of *full* salvation, *full* humanity ("holiness of heart and life"). This gift of restored power not to sin is also the work of grace and all of it is God's sheer, unmerited mercy. We can take no pride in it for ourselves. Our part is gratitude! This is the effect of Christ's ministry of reconciling love—and of a newly active presence of the Holy Spirit in our hearts, leading us toward truth and freedom and love. This creates a new syndrome of relationships (with God, ourselves, and neighbors) and all of it is the fruition of God's grace in Christ and of our response in faith, hope, and love. This response includes the recognition that we live, truly, *in* Christ and *with* Christ, and that the Christian life is a participation with Christ in his mission in the world. This means holy living and holy dying; it means a theology of the Cross *and* a theology of glory. All of this, and more, is thus implied in Wesley's quaint metaphor, "offering Christ."

Nowadays, we are finally beginning to fathom the radical shift that has taken place, and is still taking place, in the moral conscience of moderns. We can see for ourselves (we can see *in* ourselves!) the swift erosion of the old linkage between anxiety and guilt. The level of anxiety remains as high in this society as ever (maybe it is even elevated!). But, everywhere, one notices a shrinkage of any serious sense of damning *guilt before God*. The consequence of this reversal is difficult to grasp but one thing is almost self-evident: viz., the increasing irrelevance of an evangelism that is focused in the old forensic metaphor. It's no big deal nowadays to tell people that their sins are pardoned when they don't really feel *guilty* (at least not in the traditional sense), but only anxious, victimized, and put upon. Increasingly, it is not much more than "ho-hum" to proclaim that "you are accepted" to people who have already been told that they ought to have *been* accepted, by rights, *long since*. Christian evangelists must now realize that they have to find a true word of gospel for "the guiltless," those who are no longer contrite but are still nonetheless hopeless. We must seek and find a new version of the old gospel of grace and hope through Christ in the Spirit. As Richard Niebuhr might remind us, it is no gospel at all anymore (even if it ever was), to speak of "a God without wrath who brought men without sin into a kingdom without judgment through the ministrations of a Christ without a Cross." [15]

For if it is true that those who *feel* guiltless no longer need a gospel of forensic acquittal, it is also true that those who *are* hopeless need something a good deal better than "peak experiences" or extended episodes of "expanded consciousness." What kind of a gospel is it that extols freedom and happiness within the ironic brackets of transience and death? What is there to hope for if my highest aspirations are never to come to any full fruition? Are life's agonies and ecstasies really worth it after all?

Suppose we let the forensic metaphors go (as I think we may) and turn, as so many have, to therapeutic metaphors, as in the pastoral counseling movement, generally. It must be stressed that this is a definite advance, to be both welcomed and also incorporated into our theology, ethics, and so forth. But it should be obvious that *therapy,* in all of its images, connotes *amelioration* and not full self-realization of "salvation." Suppose a given therapy is *relatively* successful (which, of course, is the only way one can speak of therapy). Suppose a neurotic's repressed psychic energies are freed up and made newly available for self-expression. Suppose oppressed groups are liberated, as surely they ought to and must be. What then? Therapy or liberation or whatever are never ends in themselves. They are *means.* But means to *what end,* except lasting human joy and happiness? And what is our assurance that these ends can be attained by these means?

Beyond the courtroom and the clinic, therefore, the human hunger for happiness reaches out toward some sovereign power that really cares and is truly sovereign, that is more than a bloodless ideal or a human aspiration that is finally mocked by transcience and death. The good news we really need to hear is that "*God* so loved the world that he gave of himself to the world in order that that world [and we] might not perish [in final meaninglessness] but have eternal life [the full human potential, here and hereafter]." There's nothing forensic in this old verse and it reaches far beyond any of the current accounts I know about "peak experiences," *satori*, "cosmic consciousness," and the like. The Christian gospel is the message of God's suffering, redemptive, reconciling love that initiates a new life in Christ within the Body of Christ. "You who are justified by faith" (as St. Paul puts it) "are *in* Christ Jesus, by God's own act, for God has made him our wisdom and our righteousness [justification]; in him we are consecrated and set free" [liberated!].[16] Those for whom this is a living faith have a different ground for hope than ever they could have otherwise.

I have cited only two of the great gospel promises, two out of at least a hundred, which point to the mystery of salvation beyond any earthly self-salvation or any heavenly courtroom. They speak of a theonomous transaction, the essence of which is reconciliation between unhappy sinners and the holy God, which alters *all* the meanings of human life and death. On the human side, there are two conditions: repentance and faith. But the divine agent in the transaction is Jesus Christ, without whose redemptive love we would not have the reality of God's grace suffusing and hallowing the whole of life. It is in Christ that we find our true fulfillment in this life "and in the life of the world to come."

Human life *must* be lived in and by grace or else it will be lived gracelessly and ungraciously and death will find us not only vulnerable but literally hope-less. Autonomous humanity is foredoomed to hollow triumphs —to aspirations forever thwarted, to victories that wreak havoc and that leave the victors still unfulfilled. The gospel is God's enacted promise in Christ that we can live intentionally, following the inner leadings of the Holy Spirit, obedient to what we are given to know of God's will, growing ever into a deeper faith and a truer happiness than we could ever know, in and for and by ourselves. And Jesus Christ is the guarantor and agent of this promise, both in revealing God's love (in our human lot and all its tragedy), and in renewing our hope, in, through, and beyond tragedy. His power, shared with us, is the victory over sin and death, i.e., over their power to corrupt our faith, hope, and love. He is the enacted promise that since we *are* God's children, we can anticipate our future. Its details are shrouded; we must wait and work in faith and hope, but this much we can count on now (and in any case): "that when he shall appear, we shall be like him, and shall see him (and ourselves) as he really is (and ourselves as he meant us to become)."[17]

The Christian gospel for the guiltless is rather less that he has appeased the Father's wrath than that he is the agent of the Father's redemptive compassion. This is not at all to reject the still living truth in the grand article of justification. It is only to stress, more than our older Protestant traditions did, the theme of salvation by *participation*— in God's love in Christ through the Spirit. Our real hope lies in God's grace and in his purpose to restore such overreachers as we are to that happiness wherein human outreach (within its proper frame of dependence, trust, and obedience) does in fact achieve the happiness that God intends for his children—for *all* his children.

The gospel call is still the same: "Repent and believe

the Gospel"—the good news that God is indeed the giver of life's meanings and joys and hopes, that life in his love is ultimately secure and can even now be serene, since all its final meanings (in life *and* death) are in his hands. This is the good news: that "God is on *our* side" (Rom. 8:31). What then can separate us from the love of Christ, save unfaith or (what amounts to the same thing) self-righteousness?

In *these* terms, or something like them, the gospel is still alive and well and was never more desperately needed than by those guiltless souls whose guiltlessness has added to their final hope-lessness. *Repent* (let the Holy Spirit teach you the real truth about your sin, your need, your potential)! *Believe* the gospel, accept your radical dependence upon God's freely offered gifts of love and joy. *Go on toward holiness* (the perfect love of God and neighbor) and *expect* to be made perfect in love in this life. In such a faith and hope as this we might then look *within* with new and grace-filled insights as to God's provisions for *self*-acceptance and *self*-affirmation. We might, even at the same time, look *outward*, toward all those tasks that are prompted by human need and the imperatives of sacrificial love. And we really would be "new creatures." The old self-stultifications of life would have begun to "pass away." Can you suggest a much better definition than this of the Christian life—or, what amounts to the same thing, of *human life at its best?*

4

"HOLINESS OF HEART AND LIFE"

MOST NON-METHODISTS, and not a few Methodists, would be startled by some of the questions a Methodist ordinand is asked in the course of his "being received into full connection" (i.e., membership) in an Annual Conference. The present list[1] is a curious conflation of various examinations that Wesley devised for "admitting" his own preachers into "connexion."[2] When one recalls that these men were all laymen, it is obvious that these queries are also applicable, in principle, to any and all baptized, confirmed Christians. Their being reserved now for ordinands does not alter the fact that, for Wesley, they were appropriate clues for the examination *(self*-examination!) of all earnest Christians, to be asked and answered with unflinching seriousness.

The first one is commonplace enough. But then come three real "stickers," certainly for sensitive and knowledgeable young men and women nowadays—and for the generality of Christians of any age and station:

1. Have you faith in Christ?
2. Are you going on to perfection?
3. Do you expect to be made perfect in love in this life?[3]
4. Are you earnestly striving after it?[4]

The requisite answer, in each case, is affirmative!

All too often, in actual current circumstances (as Methodists will know from experience), these probes into the very heart of a person's Christian self-understanding are dealt with in a way that appeals to the individual interpretation of the several ordinands, few of whom have puzzled their way deeply enough into the Wesleyan doctrine of perfection to have clear and responsible commitments to what they are professing ritually. Nor is it always and altogether clear to their elders in the Conference!

There are at least two reasons for this pious confusion. The first, of course, is a widespread consensus in modern culture (instructed as we have been by depth psychology, together with an inbred cynicism) that rejects any notion of "perfection" simply out of hand and would, therefore, assess anybody's serious expectation of being "made perfect in love *in this life*" as symptomatic of a psychotic delusion. The second reason is historical and is related to the greatest tragedy in Methodist history: the nineteenth century conflicts that swirled around Wesley's emphasis upon "holiness of heart and life" and its alterations and distortions at the hands of men and women who were seeking to be faithful Wesleyans (on both sides!) without having experienced anything close to the theological and spiritual struggles out of which his own original synthesis had emerged. The ironic outcome of this process (especially in America) was that the keystone in the arch of Wesley's own theological "system" came to be a pebble in the shoes of standard-brand Methodists, even as a distorted version of Wesley's doctrine of sanctification (as "a second and separate work of grace *subsequent to* regeneration") was becoming a shibboleth of self-righteousness amongst a pious minority of Methodists who professed themselves holier than the rest. That conflict and its abrasions had the effect of leaving the average Methodist (and many much above that average) alienated even by the bare terms—"holiness," "Christian perfection," "sanctification"—not to speak of an aversion toward those persons who actually profess such spiritual attainments.

There's this occasional fantasy that sometimes crops up in my daydreaming: to set some of our curial "experts" onto a "scientific study in depth"—replete with questionnaires, computers, the whole apparatus of apparent objectivity! Their project would be to analyze a whole series of different groups in The United Methodist Church by double blinding them on these three questions about "perfection in this life" and then assessing their responses! For example: it is the bishop who asks these questions, but how many bishops still "expect to be made perfect in love in this life"? How many other Methodists expect how many bishops (and which bishops) so to be perfected? The computer would be programmed to activate a rocket for every one who claimed he already was! This would only be for starters. How many bureaucrats or journalists "are earnestly seeking after perfection"?—and how many correlations could be delineated between, say, staff people in "global ministries," "church and society," "discipleship" or wherever? How many professors and in what disciplines? How many pastors (correlated with which seminaries, and when)? How many layfolk—categorized according to age, sex, race, jurisdictions, etc., etc.? This would not be nearly as dubious and fruitless as many another solemn study project on which we have already expended unreasonable sums of money and personnel.

But I always awake from such fantasizing with a sad, grim smile—since I know as well as you that any results from this sort of thing would be doubly misleading. On the one hand, there are Methodists whom I know who are already nearer to what Wesley would have recognized as "perfection" than *they* are aware of, or would ever admit to. And, on the other hand, there are many "professors of true holiness" who come across as proud of being holier than the rest of us—and this helps to reinforce the phobias that standard-brand Methodists already have, in line with their inbred negative stereotypes. Thus, by a series of multiple ironies, the Methodists have been deprived of a vital element in their heritage and have been spiritually impoverished as a result (on *both* sides). Our traditional emphasis on "the spiritual life" is more ambiguous than it should be and our traditional commitments to social reform are less effectual. And it goes without saying that *non*-Methodists are, for the most part, baffled or unedified by this disintegration of a great tradition.

This is why the task of commenting on the theme of "holiness of heart and life" to an audience of contemporary Christians gives one the uneasy feeling that he/she *begins* by being overexposed to misunderstanding. My situation here reminds me of one of the apocryphal stories that abound in Rome about Pope John XXIII—this one before he was pope (actually when he was papal nuncio in Paris). At a banquet there for the diplomatic corps, Msgr. Roncalli was seated next to a buxom lady whose stylish gown had been designed by a minimalist (or maximalist, depending on one's viewpoint). When the fruit course was served, she declined; whereupon Msgr. Roncalli urged her to try an apple, explaining, when asked why, that it was an apple that had helped Eve to realize *her* condition!

But I take comfort and courage in such a venture from the undeniable fact that John Wesley believed and taught an explicit doctrine of "holiness" as the goal and crown of the Christian life, and if this gives you trouble, the burden of proof shifts over onto your side (if, that is, you profess to be a Wesleyan at all) to explain why you are prepared to reject or ignore what he regarded as not only essential but climactic. His irreducible minimum of Christian fundamentals were, as we have seen, three: (1) sin and repentance (i.e., self-knowledge), (2) justification and pardon (i.e., assurance) and (3) "holiness of heart and life."[5] "Sanctification," "perfect love," "Christian perfection" were various synonyms, in his vocabulary, for "holiness," and he rang the changes on this theme throughout his whole evangelistic career, insisting that it was the special mission of the Methodists to hold "and to spread [this doctrine of] scriptural holiness over the land."[6]

It is important, therefore, always to start with Wesley's first conversion (1725), a conversion to the ideal of holy living, and to remember that he never thereafter abandoned this ideal even when further conversions (and other experiences) complicated his interpretation of it by a good deal.[7] The seed of the idea had been planted in his mind in the Epworth parsonage by Susanna, one of whose favorite devotional texts was Lorenzo Scupoli's (or, as was then thought, Juan de Castaniza's) *Spiritual Struggle*.[8] The seed had flowered under the stimulus of Jeremy Taylor, Thomas à Kempis, William Law and others. But the idea of perfection as a dynamic *process* with a flying goal did not take its mature form until, finally, Wesley found his way back to the great devotional traditions of Eastern Orthodoxy—Clement of Alexandria, Gregory of Nyssa, Macarius of Egypt, and others.[9] The first fruits of these discoveries may be seen in the only great sermon of his of which we have any record before 1738. This was "The Circumcision of the Heart" (written in December of 1732 and preached in St. Mary's on January 1, 1733 [which was not New Year's Day on the then current calendar]). Too little attention has been paid to the implications of the fact that Wesley never discarded this sermon or even recast it. It turns up, in its original text but out of its chronological order, as No. XIII in *Sermons on Several Occasions*, Vol. II, 1748.[10]

It is true, that in those years, 1725–38, he consistently

misplaced "holiness" (or pure intentions) *before* justification, as preparatory to it. Bishop George Bull and most other Anglicans from Bull to Tillotson had done the same thing—and Wesley would berate them for it later on. One of the decisive shifts in his 1738 transformation was the reversal of this order. Thereafter, justification always stands first, without any antecedent "holiness" or merit of any kind as a *necessary* precondition to human salvation. Our natural sinful state can be dealt with only by God's sheer gratuitous mercy, based upon Christ's freely offered mediatorial merit. Then, and only then, can anything like new birth and Christian nurture *begin* to restore the power not to sin intentionally which may then be developed further in a nurturing process toward the goal of sanctification: "the mature man in Christ." This relation of justification to sanctification was the critical issue that had first been raised for Wesley in his encounters with the Herrnhuters and Salzburgers in Georgia. It was the main issue that divided Wesley and Whitefield almost as soon as the Revival began. It was the issue on which Wesley and Count von Zinzendorf soon clashed and finally parted.

It is easy for us to miss the originality of this Wesleyan view of faith alone and holy living *held together.* Here was a great evangelist preaching up *sola fide* and, at the very same time, teaching his converts to go on to perfection and to expect it *in this life!* His critics were quick to notice this strange move and to seize upon it as proof of Wesley's inconsistency.[11] Actually, it was yet another of Wesley's characteristic "third alternatives"—maybe his most original one. In this view, the stages of the unfolding Christian life may be laid out in something like the following sequence (a psychological sequence which was more nearly concurrent than spaced out): (1) contrition and repentance (true self-knowledge); (2) justification by faith alone (with Christ's atonement as the *meritorious* but not the *formal* cause—for, remember, this was the crux of his quarrel with the Calvinists!);[12] (3) regeneration ("new birth") issuing in (4) Christian nurture in intensive small encounter groups (with no carpets and no nonesense!); looking toward (5) maturation into "holiness," always in its twin dimensions ("internal holiness" [our *love of God* and neighbor] and "external holiness" [our love of God *and of neighbor!*]). All this was aimed at a climax (6) "perfect love" of God and neighbor as the Spirit's greatest *gift* (which means that, in Wesley's mind, sanctification *by faith alone* was as self-evident as justification ever was, never a moral achievement). And yet, as Wesley never ceased to insist, none of these "stages" is static, none of them so fully completed that one may not lapse from it by unbelief or willful sin—hence his rejection of "final perseverance." What mattered most was that "going on to perfection" has a consistent character and a clear end in view: (1) *love* (of God and neighbor), (2) *trust* (in Christ and the sufficiency of *his* grace) and (3) *joy* (joy upwelling in the heart from the "prevenience" of the indwelling Spirit). This *is* "holy living": to love God and neighbor with all your heart, to trust securely in Christ's merits, and to live joyously "in the Spirit"!

But this vital linkage between faith alone and holy living was forever being misconstrued and Wesley was forever being baffled by its misconstructions. Somehow, he could never grasp the fact that people formed by the traditions of Latin Christianity were bound to understand "perfection" as *perfectus* (perfect*ed*)—i.e., as a finished state of completed growth, *ne plus ultra!* For him, certainly since his own discoveries of the early fathers, "perfection" meant "perfect*ing*" *(teleiosis)*, with further horizons of love and of participation in God always opening up *beyond* any given level of spiritual progress. This seemed so *obvious* to him that he allowed himself a swig of smug triumphalism:

> It has been frequently observed, that [in the Reformation time] very few were clear in their judgment both with regard to justification and sanctification. Many who have spoken and written admirably well concerning justification had no clear conception, nay, were totally ignorant of the doctrine of sanctification. Who has wrote more ably than Martin Luther on justification by faith alone? And who was more ignorant of the doctrine of sanctification, or more confused in his conceptions of it? . . . On the other hand, how many writers of the Romish Church (as Francis Sales and Juan de Castaniza) have wrote strongly and scripturally on sanctification, who, nevertheless, were entirely unacquainted with the nature of justification! insomuch that the whole body of their Divines at the Council of Trent totally confound sanctification and justification together. But it has pleased God to give the Methodists a full and clear knowledge of each, and the wide difference between them.[13]

Regeneration ("new birth," "change of heart") is a concurrent effect alongside justification.[14] The sense of

God's unmerited favor prompts an inner transformation, a new disposition toward God and neighbor, a new *self-* understanding, a new outlook and hope. Even so, "this is only the threshold of sanctification. . . ." The Christian life goes on from here, in a dynamic process of nurture, piety, activity—and of *expectation:* that what is imputed in justification will be *imparted* in the Christian life and its fulfillment. *This* is "Christian perfection"—"to be made perfect in love in this life," even if only in the hour of death (which was Wesley's normal "calendar" for it).

It is, then, a great blessing given to this people, that as they do not think or speak of justification so as to supersede sanctification, so neither do they think or speak of sanctification so as to supersede justification. They take care to keep each in its own place, laying equal stress on one and the other. They know God has joined these together, and it is not for man to put down asunder. Therefore, they maintain, with equal zeal and diligence, the doctrine of free, full, present justification, on the one hand, and of entire sanctification both of heart and life, on the other; being as tenacious of *inward* holiness as any mystic, and of *outward* [holiness] as any Pharisee.

Who then is a Christian, according to the light which God hath vouchsafed to this [Methodist] people? He that, being "justified by faith, hath peace with God through our Lord Jesus Christ," and, at the same time, is "born again," "born from above," "born of the Spirit"; inwardly changed from the image of the devil, to that "image of God wherein he was created"; he that finds the love of God shed abroad in his heart by the Holy Ghost which is given unto him, and whom this love sweetly constrains to

love his neighbor (i.e., every man) as himself; he that
has learned of his Lord to be meek and lowly in heart,
and in every state to be content; he in whom is that whole
mind, all those tempers, which are also in Christ Jesus;
he that abstains from all appearance of evil in his actions,
and that offends not with his tongue; he that walks in all
the commandments of God, and in all his ordinances,
blameless; he that, in all his intercourse with men, does
to others as he would they should do to him; and in his
whole life and conversation, whether he eats or drinks, or
whatsoever he doeth, doeth all to the glory of God.[15]

This is an important version of Wesley's doctrine of
"holiness of heart and life" in his own words. Its development (apart from *this* statement) is marked out in a
series of six landmark sermons over the six-decade span
of his ministry. (1) "The Circumcision of the Heart"
which, as we have already seen, was his first full definition of the holy-living tradition. (2) "Christian Perfection" is a sermonic essay never preached, but published
first in 1741 with the express encouragement of Bishop
Edmund Gibson of London—who could tell an authentic version of the holy-living motif when he saw one.
(3) "Sin in Believers" is something of an afterthought,
added (in 1763) to correct mistaken interpretations of
"Christian Perfection," as if it implied *sinless* perfection.
It doesn't, and never did, for Wesley. (4) "The Lord Our
Righteousness" (1765) marks the decisive parting of the
ways between Wesley and the Calvinists—which is to
say, a majority of the evangelicals in the Church of
England and most Nonconformists, too. The issue, as
we have seen, is between "formal cause" and "meritori-

ous cause." This may sound like a quibble until you probe it more closely (like reading the debates at Trent[16] and Bellarmine[17] and Davenant![18]). Actually, it's the same issue as between imputation and impartation, between predestination and prevenience. "Formal cause" (to the Calvinists) implied predestination; "meritorious cause" implied God's prevenience and human synergism. The first is "protestant," the second is "catholic." And Wesley, after a full generation of evangelical preaching of justification, continues to insist that Christ's death is the *meritorious* cause of our justification but not the *formal* cause (which he takes to be God's primordial covenant that those who believe shall be saved and those who refuse shall not).

Sermon No. 5 would have to be "On Working Out Our Own Salvation" (1785), a remarkable statement of Wesley's "synergism" and, maybe, his most carefully nuanced exposition of "faith alone" and "holy living."[19] Our last sermon (6), and a fitting climax for the series, is also the last sermon published in Wesley's lifetime. Its theme is "The Wedding Garment." I had never realized until recently (after all these years of poking around, too) that this particular parable had been a sort of shibboleth between the partisans of *sola fide* and of "holy living." What *does* "the wedding garment" signify? To the Calvinists it meant the spotless robe of Christ's righteousness flung as a cover over the "filthy rags" of our *un*righteousness. To the Anglicans generally it had signified holiness itself—i.e., that Christian moral character that is attained by God's *gift* of grace and his *demand* for holy living. With death only months away, Wesley restates his basic conviction, first fixed in 1725: that "the wedding garment signifies holiness, neither more nor less"—the holiness specified in Hebrews 12:14, "without which no man shall see the Lord." Have you ever preached on this parable or heard it preached on? Have you ever considered how much this issue matters to us *today?*

Holiness as a vision of the human potential is an easily distorted notion, and you can see Wesley struggling with its misunderstandings in his *Plain Account of Christian Perfection as Believed and Taught by the Rev. Mr. John Wesley from the Year 1725 to 1765* and thereafter (six editions from 1766 to 1789). There is also that wonderful little pamphlet of 1762 entitled *Cautions and Directions Given to the Greatest Professors in the Methodist Societies,*[20] where the "professors" (i.e., of perfection) are given six highly relevant advices: (1) against pride and self-righteousness; (2) against pride's daughter, *enthusiasm* (defined as grasping for happiness without submitting oneself to its necessary preconditions); (3) against *antinomianism* (doing your own thing, regardless); (4) against sins of *omission* (getting tired and supposing that what you've already done is plenty—or at least enough); (5) against desiring anything above God, and (6) against *schism* (which, as Wesley saw it,[21] was something like pious cantankerousness!). Obviously, these "cautions and directions" were timely—prompted by more than a few rare cases of self-righteousness and spiritual elitism. Indeed, it was just this syndrome of self-righteousness amongst the holiness people that led "mainstream" Methodists finally to throw the Wesleyan baby of true holiness out with the "second blessing" bath water!

Now I don't have to tell you that, nowadays, we're in another valley of decision. New versions of "holiness," "pentecostalism," "enthusiasm," charismatic renewal, and spiritual elitism are abroad in the land, spreading the usual confusion and acrimony that seem to come along with religious revivals generally. Many United Methodist Church leaders (bishops, cathedral preachers, bureaucrats)—and leaders in other churches, too—are reacting very much like the Anglican hierarchy reacted to the Methodists in the eighteenth century. There *are* hyperpituitary Christians in our midst and they *are* divisive. But then, so also were the early Methodists! There *are* vast numbers of nominal Christians amongst us, and they are depressing. So, why should I be upset when a tongue-speaker or a Jesus freak tells me, in a patronizing tone, that I'm unsaved, or that he is holier-than-I (as several have)? Well, for one thing and obviously, my own spiritual pride and personal vanity are offended (which means, alas, that he's partially right!).

But the real tragedy is that most of us have never grasped Wesley's crucial distinction between the *extraordinary* gifts of the Spirit (healing, tongues, prophecy, discernment of spirits, teaching, and the like) and the *ordinary* fruits of the Spirit which norm everything in the Christian life, including the extraordinary gifts of the Spirit ("love, joy, peace, patience, kindness, goodness, fidelity, gentleness, and self-control"[22]). There are many people in the world whose *extraordinary* gifts of the Spirit surpass my own by a great deal, and I ought always to *rejoice* in their talents. Even so, I have the right and duty to pass judgment on them—not in terms of their "gifts" but rather their "fruits"—and they must be willing to have their gifts so judged, by the "ordinary" Christian virtues that are normative for all converted Christians. The moment one is impatient with or censorious about another's spiritual progress—or unkind, ungentle, etc., from either side (pietists denouncing the activists, activists scorning pietists, and all that!)—in *that* moment, even holy folk have backslidden into substandard Christianity, whatever their professions or rhetoric may be. Let *me* learn to rejoice in all extraordinary gifts; let *them* learn to repent of any spiritual pride they may discover in their hearts. Let us both cultivate the ordinary fruits of the Spirit and enjoy them wherever found. "If their *hearts* be as our *hearts*, let us join hands"; *this*, of course, is what Wesley meant by "catholic spirit."[23] If The United Methodist Church cannot provide as welcome a home for her right-wing Montanists as she has for her left-wing "prophets," she will have proved herself less catholic than Wesley—or St. Paul—ever supposed a church should be and still deserve the name "church" (versus a "sect").

We know (or our liberal forefathers knew) the distortions of the Wesleyan doctrine of holiness that led to its disrepute and abandonment. Wesley himself did not use the phrase, "sinless perfection"—with its simplistic view of the power not to sin—but he did not guard himself against it as carefully as he might have. And so it turned up, in the Methodist holines movement, as a shift from a notion of perfecting (or perfectible) perfection over to a claim of perfected perfection. Then came a very dubious distinction, still insisted on in holiness circles, between "a perfect heart" and "a perfect character." For example, in the current *Manual* of the Church of the Nazarene (p. 52, par. 36) such a distinction is emphasized: "The perfect heart is obtained in an instant, the result of entire sanctification, but a perfect character is the result of growth in grace." Closer home, it is fairly clear (to me, at least) that Article XI in par. 69 of the former Evangelical United Brethren Confession is closer to the nineteenth century pietist distortions of the doctrine of sanctification than to Wesley's own version of the doctrine. Either way, we have problems, *and* a signal ecumenical opportunity!

Now, I'm not about to claim to be the first man since Wesley to understand what he meant by "holiness of heart and life"—Lindstrom, Flew, Sangster, and others have probed this doctrine in considerable depth. But the fact is that modern American Methodists have relegated the whole business to the margin of their interests, as if holiness were just another of Wesley's eighteenth century crotchets, like his belief in ghosts and witchcraft. This seems to me all the more tragic because, after all my days and nights of sitting up with this strange man—hearing him and asking him questions—I've come to believe that he's *got* something that all of us need, a view that is as contemporary as transactional analysis (and much more realistic), a doctrine that is truly ecumenical: "catholic, evangelical *and* reformed." This vision of the Christian life (complex in many ways, yet quite simple at its core) might help us toward that renewal of the church that we keep talking about and praying for and are yet denied because of our partisan confusions.

What seems obvious to everyone is that Wesley was obsessed with ideas about Christian discipline and duty. His wide assortment of "rules," together with his incessant exhortations to Christian morality all combine to give us a picture of the prototypical Methodist moralist and legalist that we all know too well and have become ourselves, all too often: a church whose coat-of-arms might very well have on it a General Conference resolution rampant, over a local congregation dormant, with a Latin motto on the scroll, *Possumus non peccare* (we can stop sinning [and stop *other* people from sinning!] if only we try hard enough!). In any case, it does seem obvious that Wesley must have been a deontologist in ethics—forever asking about the *ought* in moral issues, about one's *duty* or about the rules for authentic Christian living. Now, it is generally agreed, in the history of ethics and moral theory, that deontology and Christian perfection do not mix readily. Take Kant (Wesley's younger contemporary) who was so certain that the "ought" and the "is" do not coincide in this life—ever—that, rationalist as he was, he concluded that there really must be a *heavenly* life—where duty and happiness *do coexist*, as they *ought to*.

But take a closer look at Wesley and a surprising fact emerges (at least it surprised me when I first realized what I was seeing, after all these years!). This man was a *eudaemonist*, convinced and consistent all his life. All his emphases on duty and discipline are auxiliary to his main concern for human *happiness* (blessedness, etc.).

He believed (with Aquinas, Erasmus, and Richard Lucas[24] before him) that all our truly human aspirations are oriented toward *happiness.* "The best end which any creature can pursue is happiness in God."[25] The human tragedy, therefore, is that persons seek happiness (as they *must)* but in false values that leave them unhappy, in earthly quests that leave them frustrated if unattained or unsatisfied even when attained. Wesley uses a wealth of illustrations and allusions to make this crucial point over and over again—that only misery follows false loves and false values. The world is awash with unhappiness, but always this is the effect of misplaced affections, misconceived goals, the tragic futility of self-love curving back upon itself.

In a hundred different ways, Wesley repeats the thesis: human unhappiness, in any and all its forms, comes from setting our love of creation above our love of the Creator, our love of self above our love of neighbor. But this is the generic definition of *unholiness:* innocent love corrupted by false loves. Thus he can argue that only the holy are truly happy, only the hallowed life is truly blessed, only the truly loving are actually joyful. The human potential is not self-fulfilling—and in any case it is bracketed by transience and death. All our truly human aspirations are self-transcending: they point to the love of God and neighbor as their true norms. But this is the essence of *holiness. Inward* holiness is, pre-eminently, our love of God, the love of God above all else and all else in God. *Outward* holiness is our consequent love of neighbor *(all* God's children, every accessible human being whom we may serve) with a love that springs from our love of God and that seeks the neighbor's well-being as the precondition of our own proper self-love. There's a lot of loose talk nowadays about having to love ourselves in order to be able to love others (as if this were a proper exegesis of "love your neighbor as yourself"). There *is* a grain of vital truth here: self-loathing on whatever account corrupts all our relations with all others. But there's a greater danger— and one can see it in the mounting tide of narcissism in pop-psychotherapy and in the rising vogue for public ego-trips in our pop-culture. For me to have to love myself self-consciously in order to be able to love you unself-consciously is likely to deceive us both: it gets the ends and means of our moral intentions confused. "Inward" and "outward" holiness must be integrated, into a true "wholc-i-ness."

In Wesley's case, the patterns of interrelationship are plain. In half a hundred places he sums up *"holy living," "holiness," "sanctification," "Christian perfection"* in words like these:

> What *is* religion then? It is easy to answer, if we consult the oracles of God. Accounting to these, it lies in one single point: it is neither more nor less than love. It is the love which "is the fulfilling of the law, the end of the commandment." Religion is the love of God and our neighbour; that is, every man under heaven.[26]

And this is happiness and joy, as well, the truest and most enduring joy we ever know. We have fifty-four quotes where Wesley explicitly pairs off "happy and holy" (or vice versa) and the correlation is constant throughout his works and his career.[27]

It's odd, isn't it, that for so many of us, terms like "holy" and "sanctified" sound so otherworldly, and yet we can talk about "happy" and "unhappy" with no embarrassment whatever? If I asked you if you were happy, your answer might be "yes," "no," or "somewhat," but at least you'd understand my concern. But, if I asked you how "holy" you were, you'd think I'd looped. And yet, would it be impertinent, really, for me to ask you if you do love God pre-eminently, as far as you are aware of your own best intentions? If you were willing to answer at all, then any answer you gave would reflect your ideas about "inward" holiness in Wesley's sense. And if I then could ask, "Do you love all your fellow human beings individually and collectively—i.e., are you intelligently and actively concerned for *their* well-being as far as your intentions and resources and actions are concerned?"—then any answer you gave here would expose your ideas of "outward" holiness! The sum of both answers would give us both a reliable reading as to your concept and your experience of *true happiness*.

To love God is not merely a friendly feeling toward the ground of being, nor a mood of prayer and piety toward "The Man Upstairs." It is, rather, an awareness of our radical dependence upon God's grace and our gladness that this is the truth about our lives. It means a sense of Holy Presence and of security and warmth in that Presence. It means our recognition of God's upholding love and our gratitude for his love. It means serenity in the face of death because of our confidence that God's love cannot be conquered or cancelled by death. And, most of all, it means having no other gods of our own, since the *First* Commandment is also the *last!*

But overreaching humans cannot "obey" the command to love God as simple acts of choice or even as a life program aimed at self-salvation and happiness. This is why there's so much confusion nowadays about all these self-help programs, mystical exaltations ("religious highs" and things like that), as if this sort of thing could ever be equated with authentic Christian faith and love. This is why holy living is not, strictly speaking, a human achievement or any part of sinful humanity's "natural capacity" to initiate. It is not, at bottom, part of the human potential, save in the carefully guarded sense that God's prevenient grace stimulates and enables us to respond, positively and gratefully. "We love *him* because he first loved *us.*" It is God's *initiative* that makes possible our *response;* it is his *self*-presentation in Christ that frees us to accept his acceptance of us. It is his saving work in our justification that liberates us for valid ethical endeavor: in our personal maturations in grace and in our involvements in all effective transformations of society under the aegis of the Kingdom of God.

Thus "faith alone" remains as the threshold of all true holiness in heart and life—and of human happiness— here and hereafter. Wesley analyzes this in a remarkable trio of sermons on "The Law Established Through Faith."[28] Faith stands first *(sola fide)* but not as an end in itself. Nor is it a meritorious *act,* as many fundamentalists seem to insist. Rather, faith is a means in order to *love* just as love is in order to *goodness,* just as goodness is in order to *happiness*—which is what God made us for, in this world—and the next. *This* is "holy living."

Likewise, our love of neighbor (if it ever becomes more than benevolent feeling) follows from our love of God. Love of neighbor is a function of our concern to hallow *all* of life, in all of its occasions, great and small. It is our part in answering the Lord's prayer, "Thy Kingdom come, thy will *be done on earth. . . .*" [Why *can't* we ever get that punctuation right? The comma belongs after *"on earth,"* not before!] In any case, I'd feel easier with my pietist friends if their neighborly love were not so self-selective of their own kind. I'd feel easier about my activist colleagues if their neighborly love weren't so often ruthless. The only love I've ever known that I've trusted and felt sustained by was *from* God, *through* men and women whose love was unselfish—i.e., people who have loved me grace-fully. This indeed is what I *mean* by love—and all of us have been blessed by it, most of us far beyond our deservings or gratitude. It is grace-filled love that helps us become human and that nourishes our humanity.

This is why there was so much *joy* in Wesley(and in the best Wesleyan traditions of holiness of heart and life) —so much happiness in a man who had been taught from infancy to hold his emotions in check and whose temperament was remarkably cool (even amidst the violent emotions he managed to stir up). He was not an exuberant type and he deplored all flippancy and small talk. This is one reason why he has been easier for me to study than he would have been to live and work with. And yet, there *is* this strange, insistent reality of cheerfulness and high spirits that keeps breaking through his knit-browed earnestness. He was, I've come finally to realize, a happy man, in his own sense of "happiness": the human affects of loving God and serving others. And this joyousness of his (and of his brother Charles even more) was infectious. It became a part of the Methodist tradition, its hymnody, its distinctive lifestyle. Some of it still continues in our current tradition—sometimes trivialized, often faked. But what a wonder it would be if we could recover such a tradition's inner springs: viz., the grace of our Lord Jesus Christ who is the Father's redemptive love making life holy and happy, in and by the power of the Holy Spirit in our hearts! *Then,* we'd have no more trouble with those questions about going on to perfection, etc.! *Are* you? Yes, by God's grace! Then, right on! Praise the Lord!

Wesley died happy—singing and praying. The particular hymn that came to him on that last day was already a favorite with all those people in that little room in the house on City Road. It was by Isaac Watts—a sort of poetic comment on the "art of holy *dying*" that Wesley had so long taught his people as the converse of "the art of holy *living*." "I'll praise my Maker while I've breath. . . ." What we can see now, I hope, is that this was a reiteration, *in extremis,* of what Wesley had always said the breath of life is for—and what it had been for, for him, throughout his whole incredible career. God *has* made us for himself. Our first and last end *is* to love him, and to *enjoy him* forever. This *is* holiness of heart and life, and it was Wesley's witness in life *and* death. It was, therefore, a last reprise of the theme of that first conversion, long ago:

> I'll praise my Maker while I've breath
> And, when my voice is lost in death,
> Praise shall employ my *nobler* powers.
> My days of praise shall *ne'er* be past,
> While life *and* thought *and* being last,
> And immortality endures.

Amen!

NOTES

1. "PLUNDERING THE EGYPTIANS"

1. "The Denman Lectures on Evangelism," New Orleans, Louisiana, January 4–8, 1971 (Nashville, Tennessee: Tidings, 1971).

2. Cf. Bernard Semmel, *The Methodist Revolution* (New York: Basic Books, Inc., 1973).

3. Cf. James Boswell, *Life of Johnson* (3d ed.; 1799), Tuesday, March 31, 1778. Cf. also Wednesday, April 15, 1778, and Tuesday, July 13, 1779.

4. Cf. John Wesley, *A Concise History of England. From the Earliest Times to the Death of George II*. In four volumes (London, 1776 [only the last volume is dated]).

5. Cf. *A Survey of the Wisdom of God in the Creation: or a Compendium of Natural Philosophy*. First edition in two volumes, 1763; second edition in three volumes, 1770; third edition, "enlarged," in *five* volumes, 1777.

6. Cf. "On Christian Doctrine (*De Doctrina Christiana*), ch. xi, entitled, "Whatever has been rightly said by the heathen, we must appropriate to our own uses."

7. "Moreover, if those who are called philosophers (and especially the Platonists) have said aught that is true and in harmony with our faith, we are not only not to shrink from it but to claim it for our own use." *Idem*, par. 60.

90

8. In his diaries, letters, *Journal*, etc.

9. *Ad populum,* as he says quaintly, in the preface to *Sermons on Several Occasions* (London, 1746).

10. Cf., e.g.,

> *Post ignem aetherea domo*
> *Subductum, macies et nova febrium*
> *Terris incubuit cohors; . . .*

from *Odes*, Book I, iii. Ins. 29–31. In his sermon on "God's Approbation of His Works," II. 1, in *The Works of John Wesley*, edited by Thomas Jackson (London 1729–31), VI, pp. 213–14 (hereafter cited as *Works*), Wesley paraphrases these lines, ". . . in plain English, after man, in utter defiance of his Maker, had eaten of the tree of knowledge . . . a whole army of evils, totally new, totally unknown till then, broke in upon rebel man, and all other creatures, and overspread the face of the earth." In his sermon "The Heavenly Treasure in Earthen Vessels," II. 1 *(Works*, VII, p. 346), he gives another version, "After man had stolen fire from heaven (what an emblem of forbidden knowledge!) that unknown army of consumptions, fevers, sickness, pain of every kind, fixed their camp upon earth. . . ."

See also, *Si possis, recte; si non, quocunque modo rem,* from Horace's *Epistles,* I. 1. 66. In the sermon "On the Education of Children," par. 19 *(Works,* VII, p. 95), Wesley translates, "Get money, honestly if you can; but if not, get money." In "National Sins and Miseries," II. 2 *(Works,* VII, p. 405), he translates, "If you can get money honestly, do; but however, get money." Cf. also the sermon on "The Danger of Riches," par. 1 *(Works,* VII, p. 1) where, without Horace's Latin, Wesley says, "They that will be rich, that is, will be rich at all events, will be rich, right or wrong."

11. Cf., e.g., *The Aeneid*, Book VI, Ins. 726–27: "*Totam,/Mens agitans molem, et magno se corpore miscens, . . .*" ("The all-

informing soul, that fills, pervades, and actuates the whole"),
which Wesley quotes in his sermons "Of the Church," par. 13
(Works, VI, p. 395) ; "Spiritual Worship," I.5 *(Works,* VI, p. 427),
and "On the Omnipresence of God," II. 1 *(Works,* VII, p. 240).
See also his *The Doctrine of Original Sin, According to Scripture,
Reason and Experience,* Part I, par. I. 13 *(Works,* IX, p. 203).

12. Aristophanes, Hadrian, Homer, Lucanus, Lucretius, Persius,
Pindar, Seneca, Sophocles, Suetonius, Terence, Velleius Paterculus.

13. In his letter to the Mayor of Newcastle-upon-Tyne, October 26,
1745, *The Letters of John Wesley,* edited by John Telford (London: Epworth Press, 1931), II, p. 52 (hereafter cited as *Letters).*
See also *The Journal of John Wesley,* edited by Nehemiah Curnock (London: Robert Cully, 1909–1916), III, p. 217 (hereafter
cited as *Journal).*

14. Cf. his *Primitive Physick* in its twenty-three editions between
1747 and 1791; remember also his pioneer use of "electrification"
as a therapeutic procedure.

15. Thomas Otway (1652–1685), student of Christ Church before
Wesley, wrote two very popular tragedies *(The Orphan* and *Venice
Preserv'd* [1682]). Oliver Goldsmith thought Otway was, "next to
Shakespeare, the greatest genius England has ever produced in
tragedy." Earlier, Richard Steele, in *The Conscious Lovers,* Act II,
Sc. 2, had also ranked Otway with Shakespeare.

16. Curator, Methodist Historical Collection, Bridwell Library

17. *Letters,* IV, p. 299. On February 5, 1756, in a letter to William Dodd *(Letters,* III, p. 156), Wesley had written that he
"began to make the Scriptures my study (about seven and twenty
years ago)."

18. This phrase has a curious history. Wesley got it in this form
from Jeremy Taylor, *Life of Christ,* Part ii., Section 12, Discourse

XII, par. 16 in *The Works of Jeremy Taylor*, I, p. 230, but its more common usage was quite opposite: *Cavete hominem unius libri* ("beware of a man of just one book")—i.e., anybody who relies inordinately on a single authority. Archbishop John Tillotson, in his sermon on Luke 16:8, "Wiser Than the Children of Light," says, "It is a saying, I think of Thomas Aquinas, *Cave ab illo qui unicum legit librum:* 'He is a dangerous man that reads but one book' " *(Sermons* [1722], I, p. 565). Despite the legend that this monition goes back to St. Thomas Aquinas, it appears in none of his published writings. More probably, its source was Roger Bacon's complaint against the servile citations of Peter Lombard's *Sentences* as a sufficient authority in settling disputed theological questions. Cf. Bacon, *Opus minus* in *Opera quaedam hactenus inedita*, I, pp. 328–29 (1859).

19. Cf. *Journal*, I, p. 447 (Tuesday, March 23, 1738) : "I began the Greek Testament again, resolving to abide by 'the law and the testimony'; and being confident that God would hereby show me whether this doctrine was of God." See also *Letters*, III, p. 332, for his letter to William Law, January 6, 1756: "In every point I appeal 'to the law and the testimony,' and value no authority but this." In his sermon on "The Nature of Enthusiasm," par. 22 *(Works,* V, pp. 473–74), Wesley says we should seek to know and do "the will of God" not by *"particular impressions"* but by appeals "to the law and the testimony."

20. Cf., e.g., *Journal*, III, p. 17; Wesley's sermon on the "Sermon on the Mount, XII," III. 9 *(Works,* V, p. 421) ; and "Catholic Spirit," III. 2 *(Works,* V, p. 502).

21. "Original Sin," par. 4 *(Works,* VI, p. 55).

20. Cf., e.g., *Journal*, III, p. 17; Wesley's sermon on the "Sermon on the Mount, XII," III. 9 *(Works,* V, p. 421) ; and "Catholic Spirit," III. 2 *(Works,* V, p. 502).

23. Cf. Albert C. Outler (ed.), *John Wesley* in A LIBRARY OF PROTESTANT THOUGHT (New York: Oxford University Press, 1964),

pp. 146–47 (hereafter cited as LPT *Wesley*): "Q. 14. What books may an Assistant read? A. Sallust, Caesar, Tully, Erasmus, Castellio, Terence, Virgil, Horace, Vida, Buchanan, G. Test., Epictetus, Plato, Ignatius, Ephraim Syrus, Homer, *Greek Epigrams*, Duport, Bp. Ussher's *Sermons*, Arndt, Boehm, Nalson, Pascal, Francke, R. Gell, our *Tracts*." See also *Minutes of Several Conversations (Works*, VIII, p. 315) where Wesley admonishes reluctant students, "Contract a taste for reading by use or return to your trade."

24. Cf. *Works*, X, pp. 480–500.

2. DIAGNOSING THE HUMAN FLAW

1. Cf. his letter to George Downing, April 6, 1761 *(Letters*, IV, p. 146) and his letter to "Various Clergymen," April 19, 1764) *(Letters*, IV, p. 237).

2. Cf. Article VII, "Of Original or Birth Sin," in *The Book of Discipline of The United Methodist Church, 1972*, par. 69, p. 55, where Wesley's abridgment of Article IX of the "Thirty-Nine Articles" of the *Book of Common Prayer* reads as follows: "Original sin standeth not in the following of Adam (as the Pelagians do vainly talk), but in the corruption of the nature of every man, that naturally is engendered of the offspring of Adam, whereby man is very far gone from original righteousness, and of his own nature inclined to evil, and that continually."

See also the former Evangelical United Brethren "Confession," Article VII, "Sin and Free Will," ibid., pp. 62–63: "We believe man is fallen from righteousness and, apart from the grace of our Lord Jesus Christ, is destitute of holiness and inclined to evil. Except a man be born again, he cannot see the Kingdom of God. In his own strength, without divine grace, man cannot do good influenced and empowered by the Holy Spirit is responsible in works pleasing and acceptable to God. We believe, however, man freedom to exercise his will for good."

3. The so-called "Five Points of Calvinism" were easily remembered by their acronym:

1. T-otal Depravity
2. U-nconditional Election
3. L-imited Atonement
4. I-rresistible Grace
5. P-erseverance of the Saints

4. For the details, cf. the important account of this controversy, from an "evangelical" perspective, in C. F. Allison, *The Rise of Moralism: The Proclamation of the Gospel from Hooker to Baxter* (New York: Seabury Press, 1966).

5. Philip Schaff, *Creeds of Christendom* (New York: Harper & Brothers, 1882), III, pp. 523–24. For the account of this affair that Wesley himself knew best, see Jeremy Collier, *An Ecclesiastical History of Great Britain* (London, 1714), II, pp. 644–45.

6. Romans 7:21–23.

7. For example, cf. "Remarks on Mr. Hill's Review" *(Works,* X, p. 403): ". . . I did not see clearly that we are saved by faith till the year 1738. . . ." Also his letter to William Law *(Letters,* I, pp. 239–42), dated May 14, 1738, where Wesley sharply criticizes his old mentor for not having "advised" him of "this living, justifying faith in the blood of Jesus." In his "Farther Appeal . . ." *(Works,* VIII, p. 111), Wesley says he was ordained deacon in 1725 and "during all that time I was utterly ignorant of justification and confounded by sanctification. . . ." In one of his last sermons, "On the Wedding Garment," par. 18 *(Works,* VII, p. 317), he says, "Only about fifty years ago [i.e., 1738–40] I had a clearer view than before of justification by faith—and in this time, from that very hour, I never varied. . . ."

8. Summarized, from the *sola fide side,* in Allison, *Rise of Moralism,* chs. 1, 3, 4, 8.

9. Job 3:17, "There the Wicked," October 1, 1725;

Matthew 6:33, "Seek Ye First," November 21, 1725;

Psalm 91:11, "On Guardian Angels," September 29, 1726;

2 Samuel 12:23, "On Mourning for the Dead," January 11, 1727;

2 Corinthians 2:17, "On Corrupting the Word of God," October 6, 1727;

John 1:47, "On Dissimulation," January 17, 1728;

Exodus 20:8, "On the Sabbath," July 4, 1730;

John 13:7, "What I Do, Thou Canst Not Know," October 13, 1730;

Genesis 1:27, "The Image of God," November 1, 1730;

Proverbs 11:30, "He That Winneth Souls is Wise," July 12, 1731;

Amos 3:6, "Public Diversions," n.d. (probably ca. 1732);

Mark 12:30, "Love of God and Neighbour," September 15, 1733;

Luke 16:8, "Wiser Than the Children of Light," n.d.;

Matthew 6:22, 23, "A Single Intention," February 3, 1736;

1 Corinthians 13:3, "On Love," February 20, 1736;

Isaiah 1:21, "Hypocrisy in Oxford" (English text), June 24, 1741; (Latin text), June 27, 1741.

10. *Pugna Spiritualis* (1599); cf. Lawrence Scupoli, *The Spiritual Combat and a Treatise on Peace of the Soul* (Philadelphia: The Westminster Press, 1945).

11. Edited by Winthrop S. Hudson (Philadelphia: The Westminster Press, 1948).

12. *Journal*, I, pp. 418–20.

13. Ibid., pp. 458–59.

14. Ibid., pp. 475–77.

15. Ibid., II, pp. 3–63.

16. Ibid., pp. 83–84.

17. "In the following week I began more narrowly to inquire what the doctrine of the Church of England is concerning the

much-controverted point of justification by faith; and the sum of what I found in the Homilies I extracted and printed for the use of others." Ibid., p. 101.

18. Ibid., p. 125.

19. In his letter to John Newton, May 14, 1765 *(Letters,* IV, p. 298).

20. Wesley's doctrine of Christian perfection is an amalgam of many sources, but its fountainhead (outside the New Testament, of course) is Gregory of Nyssa; cf. LPT *Wesley,* pp. 9–10, note 26.

21. Cf. Peter Heylyn, *Historia Quinquarticularis* (1659), and Collier, *Ecclesiastical History.*

22. W. E. H. Lecky, *A History of England in the Eighteenth Century,* New Edition (London: Longmans, Green, and Co., 1892), III, p. 122.

23. Cf. the doctrinal guidelines specified in the new "Doctrinal Statement," included in *The Discipline of The United Methodist Church, 1972,* Part II, par. 70, pp. 75ff.

24. "Original Sin," III.5 *(Works,* VI, p. 64).

25. *The Principles of a Methodist Farther Explained (Works,* VIII, pp. 472–73).

26. Cf. Wesley's sermon "On Wandering Thoughts" (1760+). This sermon did not appear in the first edition of Vol. III of *Sermons on Several Occasions* (1750). It *did* appear, however, in the second edition, inserted between "Christian Perfection" and "Satan's Devices" as No. XII in Vol. III—and in the series is numbered XXXVI. This second edition bears no date. See E. H. Sugden, *The Standard Sermons of John Wesley* (London: Epworth Press, 1956), II, pp. 178–90.

27. "On Sin in Believers" (March 28, 1763), No. XLVI, ibid., pp. 360–78.

28. Cf. "The Scripture Way of Salvation," III.6, ibid., p. 454. See also, "The Deceitfulness of the Human Heart," II.5 *(Works,* VII, 341) : ". . . the heart, even of a believer, is not wholly purified when he is justified. Sin is then overcome but it is not rooted out; it is conquered, but not destroyed."

29. Cf. "Large Minutes" (1744), p. 2: "If a believer wilfully sins, he casts away his faith . . . for a man may forfeit the free gift of God, either by sins of omission or commission."

30. Cf. Exodus 13:3, 14; 20:2; Deuteronomy 5:6; 6:12; 8:14; 13:5, 10; Joshua 24:17; Judges 6:8.

31. Romans 8:15.

32. 2 Thessalonians 2:7.

33. 1 Timothy 3:16.

3. ON "OFFERING CHRIST"

1. Chapter 1, p. 13.

2. *Journal,* II, p. 243.

3. Cf. the "Large Minutes" (1744), I, p. 99, "Q. 10. What is the best general method in preaching? A. (1) To invite; (2) to convince; (3) to offer Christ; (4) to build up—and to do this, in some measure, in every sermon."

4. *Journal,* I, p. 476.

5. Paul Tillich, *The Shaking of the Foundations* (New York: Charles Scribner's Sons, 1948), p. 162. Cf. Alan Walker, *Jesus the Liberator* (Nashville: Abingdon Press, 1973), p. 47.

6. Cf. Peter Gay, *The Weimar Culture* (New York: Harper & Row, 1968), for a brilliant account of the culture in which Tillich grew into maturity; see also Hannah Tillich, *From Time to Time* (New York: Stein and Day, 1973), for a libellous account of how Professor Tillich responded to the stimuli of his "liberation."

7. *Journal*, II, p. 467.

8. This turning point may be seen in his sermon, "The Lord Our Righteousness" (1765), No. XLIX, Sugden, *Standard Sermons*, II, pp. 420–41.

9. Cf. *Cur Deus Homo* (1097).

10. Cf. Romans 1:17; 3:5, 21–26, 30; 5:1; 6:7, etc.

11. Cf. No. V, Sugden, *Standard Sermons*, I, pp. 112–30.

12. Cf. No. L, ibid., II, pp. 442–60.

13. Ibid., I, p. 120.

14. Ibid., pp. 120–21.

15. Richard Niebuhr, *The Kingdom of God in America* (Chicago: Willett, Clark and Company, 1937), p. 193.

16. Cf. 1 Corinthians 1:24–30, which, as we saw, was Wesley's favorite text for 1739.

17. John 3:2. Wesley records that he preached on this text (and context) eighteen times altogether.

4. "HOLINESS OF HEART AND LIFE"

1. In *The Book of Discipline, 1972*, par. 334.

2. The primary texts may be seen in "The Large Minutes" (1766), chiefly from the Leeds Conference of 1766, but with bits and pieces from the first Conference (at the Foundery, 1744), and from "The Twelve Rules of a Helper" (1763). Cf. *Works*, VIII, pp. 309–10.

3. Wesley's text: "Do you expect to be perfected in love in this life?" ("The Large Minutes," 1766, p. 54).

4. Wesley's text: "Are you groaning after it?"

5. See above, p. 23; also chapter 2, note 1.

6. Cf. "Minutes of Several Conversations Between the Rev. Mr. Wesley and Others From the Year 1744 to the Year 1789," *Works*, VIII, p. 299.

7. Cf. Wesley's recollection of this conversion, its substance and consequences in *A Plain Account of Christian Perfection*, pars. 2–6 (1766).

8. See above, p. 31.

9. Cf. LPT *Wesley*, p. 31. Also, see above, chapter 2, note 19.

10. Notice his affirmative retrospect of it in *A Plain Account of Christian Perfection*, par. 6, where he says (in 1766) that he had *continued* in this in this view of "holy living," "without any material addition or diminution."

11. Cf. Josiah Tucker, *A Brief History of the Principles of Methodism* (Oxford, 1742).

12. In Wesley's view, the formal cause of our justification is God's *mercy*; cf. his pamphlet, *Thoughts on the Imputed Righteousness of Christ* (1762), in *Works*, X, pp. 312–15.

13. "On God's Vineyard," I.5 *(Works,* VII, p. 204) ; cf. notes on this passage (including the reference to Castaniza) in LPT *Wesley,* pp. 107–8.

14. This goes back to Melanchthon's famous *causa concurrens,* and to Bucer's *iustitia duplex* (both of them indebted to Erasmus). It was one of the Bucer-Gropper formulae in *The Book of Ratisbon* (1545) ; it was advocated by Pole and Seripando at Trent, and also by Bellarmine in the *De Auxillis* controversy. It was one of Cranmer's points in the Homilies which Wesley abridged in his *Doctrine of Salvation, Faith and Good Works* (1738). In short, this is the "catholic" obverse to the "protestant" *sola fide.*

15. "On God's Vineyard," I.8, 9 *(Works,* VII, pp. 205–6).

16. Hubert Jedin, "The Opening of the Debate on Justification," in *A History of the Council of Trent* (London: Thomas Nelson, 1961), Vol. II, ch. v, pp. 166–96, and especially the draft decree on justification produced by Girolamo Seripando, pp. 239ff.

17. Cf. Robert Bellarmine's discussion of the "causes of the justification of the impious" in his *De justificatione,* I, ii., in *De Controversiis Christianae Adversus Huius Temporis Haereticas* (Ingolstadt, 1601), IV, p. 935—especially his comments on "meritorious cause."

18. Cf. Allison, *Rise of Moralism,* chs. 1, 3, 5, 7, 8.

19. It may be read in *Works,* VI, pp. 506–13.

20. Cf. LPT *Wesley,* pp. 298–305.

21. Cf. the Sermon "On Schism," in *Works,* VI, pp. 401–10.

22. Cf. Galatians 5:22.

23. Cf. his sermon under this title in LPT *Wesley*, pp. 91–102.

24. Cf. Richard Lucas, *Enquiry After Happiness* (London, 1717), which Wesley read while at Oxford (1730 and following) with evident appreciation. See V.H.H. Green, *The Young Mr. Wesley* (London: Edward Arnold, 1961), pp. 131, 132, 155, 196.

25. As he says in "The Righteousness of Faith," II.9, Sugden, *Standard Sermons*, I, p. 143.

26. "The Important Question," III.2 *(Works*, VI, p. 498).

27. Martin Schmidt has recognized this without quite approving it. Cf. his *John Wesley: A Theological Biography* (Nashville: Abingdon, 1973), II[2], p. 214: "'holiness and happiness' was a formula which had seized and activated him from his youth up." On the following page (215), Schmidt repeats himself: "'Holiness and happiness' is [Wesley's] favorite formula."

28. Cf. "The Original, Nature, Property, and Use of the Law," "The Law Established Through Faith, I," and "The Law Established Through Faith, II," in Sugden, *Standard Sermons*, II, pp. 37–83.